Dante and His Circle

including Dante's
Vita Nuova

poems by
Giani Alfani
Dante Alighieri
Cecco Angiolieri
Simone dell' Antelle
Giovanni Boccaccio
Bernardo da Bologna
Onesto di Boncima
Giotto di Bondone
Terino da Castel Fiorentino
Guido Cavalcanti
Dino Compagni
Forese Donati
Dino Frescobaldi
Lapo Gianni
Guido Guinicelli
Dante da Maiano
Guido Orlandi
Cino da Pistoia

translator Dante Gabriel Rossetti

editor Sasha Newborn

BANDANNA BOOKS   2012   SANTA BARBARA

DANTE AND HIS CIRCLE, INTRODUCTION copyright © 1993 Bandanna Books
ISBN 0-942208-09-9   www.bandannabooks.com   Third printing 2013

MUDBORN PRESS

First Person Intense   The Basement   Eight 2 Two
Italian for Opera Lovers   French for Food Lovers   Pi for Math Lovers

BANDANNA BOOKS

Don't Panic: The Procrastinator's Guide to Writing an Effective Term Paper.
The First Detective: 3 Stories. Edgar Allan Poe   Gandhi on the *Bhagavad Gita*
The Everlasting Gospel, William Blake   **Frankenstein,** Mary Shelley
Dante and His Circle. Love sonnets   **Vita Nuova,** Dante on Beatrice
Ghazals of Ghalib   **The Gospel According to Tolstoy**
  Hadji Murad, a Chechen story, Leo Tolstoy
Mitos y Leyendas/Myths and Legends of Mexico. Bilingual
The Beechers Through the 19th Century
Uncle Tom's Cabin, H.B. Stowe   **Aurora Leigh,** E.B. Browning

TEACHING SUPPLEMENTS

(Q and A, glossaries, critical comments)
Areopagitica, John Milton   **Apology of Socrates & The Crito,** Plato
Leaves of Grass, Walt Whitman   **Sappho, The Poems**
Uncle Tom's Cabin, Harriet Beecher Stowe

SHAKESPEARE FOR DIRECTORS, PRODUCERS, ACTORS, WANNABEES

DIRECTOR'S PLAYBOOK SERIES. the elements of production: storyboarding, auditions, staging diagrams, budget, publicity, costuming, set design, playbill, stage managing, glossary, customized actor scripts

Hamlet   The Merchant of Venice   Twelfth Night   Taming of the Shrew
A Midsummer Night's Dream   Romeo and Juliet   As You Like It   Richard III
Henry V   Much Ado About Nothing   Macbeth   Othello
plus
7 Plays with Transgender Characters   Falstaff: Four Plays   Venus and Adonis

Contents

Introduction 7
LOVE AND THE LADIES
Lappo's Lady

Lappo Gianni, *what Love shall provide*	19
Guido Cavalcanti, *in a feigned vision*	20
Dante Alighieri, *a pleasant voyage*	20
Guido Cavalcanti, *speaking with shame*	21
Guido Cavalcanti, *mistrusts the love of Lappo Gianni*	21
Lappo Gianni, *for his lady Lagia*	22
Guido Cavalcanti, *detection of a false friend*	23

Cecco's Lady

Cecco Angiolieri, *Becchina, the shoemaker's daughter*	24
Cecco Angiolieri, *Becchina, and her husband*	25
Cecco Angiolieri, *in absence from Becchina*	25
Guido Cavalcanti, *a newly enriched man*	26
Cecco Angiolieri, *rails against Dante*	26
Cecco Angiolieri, *of Love*	27
Cecco Angiolieri, *of the 20th June 1291*	27

Cavalcanti and Various Ladies

Guido Cavalcanti, *compares all things with his lady*	28
Guido Cavalcanti, *his lady among other ladies*	29
Guido Cavalcanti, *his lady Joan, of Florence*	29
Guido Cavalcanti, *a rapture*	30
Guido Cavalcanti, *eyes of a certain Mandetta*	30
Guido Cavalcanti, *increasing love for Mandetta*	31
Gianni Alfani, *a lady of Pisa*	33
Bernardo da Bologna, *a certain Pinella*	33
Guido Cavalcanti, *commending Pinella*	34
Guido Cavalcanti, *a shepherd maid*	34
Guido Cavalcanti, *pain from a new love*	35
Guido Orlandi, *finds fault with the conceits*	36
Dino Compagni, *reproves Guido for his arrogance*	37
Guido Cavalcanti, *a third love*	37
Guido Cavalcanti, *an ill-favored lady*	38

Guido Cavalcanti, *a friend who does not pity*	38
Guido Cavalcanti, *a continual death in love*	39

An Assortment of Ladies

Guido Guinicelli, *will praise his lady*	40
Dante Alighieri, *will gaze upon Beatrice*	41
Guido Cavalcanti, *praise of Guido Orlandi's lady*	41
Guido Orlandi, *his lady's champion*	42
Onesto de Boncima, *wish to meet his lady alone*	42
Terino da Castel, *answer to the foregoing*	43
Dante da Maiano, *his lady Nina, of Sicily*	43
Dante da Maiano, *thanks his lady for the joy*	44
Guido Guinicelli, *concerning Lucy*	44
Dante Alighieri, *on All Saints' Day*	45
Dino Frescobaldi, *what his lady is*	45
Dino Frescobaldi, *star of his love*	46
Cino da Pistoia, *to his lady Selvaggia Vergiolesi*	46
Cino da Pistoia, *Death is not without*	47

Cecco's Father

Cecco Angiolieri, *to Messer Angiolieri, his father*	48
Cecco Angiolieri, *concerning his father*	49
Cecco Angiolieri, *his four tormentors*	49
Cecco Angiolieri, *death of his father*	50
Cecco Angiolieri, *slay all who hate their fathers*	50

Affairs of the Heart

Dante Alighieri, *of beauty and duty*	51
Guido Guinicelli, *of the gentle heart*	52
Cecco Angiolieri, *not too deeply in love*	54
Guido Cavalcanti, *presumption of his youth*	54
Cino da Pistoia, *Love, in great bitterness*	55
Dante Alighieri, *rebukes Cino for fickleness*	55
Cino da Pistoia, *confessing his unsteadfast heart*	56
Guido Guinicelli, *of moderation and tolerance*	56
Cecco Angiolieri, *love in men and devils*	57
Guido Guinicelli, *rashness in love*	58

Dreams and Images

Cino da Pistoia, *trance of Love*	60
Dante da Maiano, *interpreting of a dream*	61
Guido Orlandi, *he interprets the dream*	61
Cecco Angiolieri, *of all he would do*	62
Guido Cavalcanti, *image resembling his lady*	62
Guido Orlandi, *answer to the foregoing*	63

Vita Nuova

Sonnet to Brunetto Latini	66
To every heart which the sweet pain does move	70
All you that pass along Love's trodden way	73
Weep, lovers, since Love's very self does weep	74
Death, always cruel, Pity's foe in chief	75
A day agone, as I rode sullenly	77
Song, 'tis my will that you do seek out Love	81
All my thoughts always speak to me of Love	84
Even as the others mock, you mock me	87
The thoughts are broken in my memory	89
At whiles (yea oftentimes) I muse over	90
Ladies that have intelligence in love	93
Love and the gentle heart are one same thing	96
My lady carries love within her eyes	97
You that thus wear a modest contenance	99
Can you indeed be he that still would sing	100
A very pitiful lady, very young	103
I felt a spirit of love begin to stir	107
My lady looks so gentle and so pure	111
Fer certain he has seen all perfectness	112
Love has so long possessed me for his own	113
The eyes that weep for pity of the heart	116
Stay now with me, and listen to my sighs	119
Whatever while the thought comes over me	121
That lady of all gentle memories	123
My eyes beheld the blessed pity spring	124
Love's pallor and the semblance of deep remorse	125
The very bitter weeping that you made	126
A gentle thought there is will often start	128
Woe's me! by force of all these sighs that come	130
You pilgrim folk, advancing pensively	132
Beyond the sphere which spreads to widest space	133

Works

Beatrice's Death and After

Dante Alighieri, *on the 9th of June 1290*	136
Dante Alighieri, *he beseeches Death*	137
Cino da Pistoia, *some compensation in death*	139
Giovanni Boccaccio, *after Fiammetta's death*	140

Cino da Pistoia, *death of Beatrice Portinari*	140
Guido Cavalcanti, *rebukes Dante for his way of life*	141
Dante Alighieri, *to the lady Pietra degli Scrovigni*	141
Dante Alighieri, *of the lady Pietra degli Scrovigni*	142

On Death

Guido Guinicelli, *of human presumption*	143
Cecco Angiolieri, *Gramercy, Death*	144
Guido Cavalcanti, *his highest love is gone*	144
Dante Alighieri, *when Beatrice was lamenting*	145
Dante Alighieri, *with their answer*	146
Onesto di Boncima, *of the Last Judgment*	146
Cino da Pistoia, *of the grave of Selvaggia*	147
Cino da Pistoia, *his lament for Selvaggia*	147
Guido Cavalcanti, *a dispute with Death*	149

On Poverty

Giotto di Bondone, *doctrine of voluntary poverty*	158
Guido Cavalcanti, *a song against poverty*	154
Cecco Angiolieri, *he is past all help*	156
Guido Cavalcanti, *a Song of Fortune*	157
Cecco Angiolieri, *why he would be a scullion*	159
Cecco Angiolieri, *why he is unhanged*	160

Controversies and Politics

Cino da Pistoia, *he owes nothing to Guido*	161
Giovanni Boccaccio, *to one who had censured him*	162
Guido Cavalcanti, *In exile at Sarzana*	162
Cecco Angiolieri, *Dante as no better than himself*	164
Dante Alighieri, *he taunts Forese*	164
Forese Donati, *he taunts Dante ironically*	165
Dante Alighieri, *He taunts him concerning his wife*	165
Forese Donati, *unavenged spirit of Geri Alighieri*	166
Guido Cavalcanti, *after the Pope's Interdict*	166
Guido Orlandi, *against the "White" Ghibellines*	167
Simone dall' Antella, *last days of Emperor Henry VII*	167

Index of First Lines	168
Glossary	177

Introduction

AS A YOUNG POET, Dante Alighieri was at the center of a new attitude sweeping through Italy and southern France. Poets and artists were awakening from a thousand-year yoke we now call the Middle Ages. Giotto showed the way in art by painting real people in his allegorical scenes; Dante used vernacular or street language to write down his actual feelings. And a new subject drove these and other passionate artists: Love.

Who were the poets of Dante's circle? This edition of *Dante and His Circle* is based upon an imaginative recreation of a cultural and intellectual ferment at the birth of a national literature. Dante Gabriel Rossetti brought together poetry of the friends and antagonists of Dante—in particular the poems of the flamboyant Guido Cavalcanti, the staid Cino da Pistoia, and the outrageous Cecco Angiolieri, with many others—and including the curious work of the youthful Dante called the *Vita Nuova* (The New Life, or My Young Life; available separately), which itself is the subject of comments by Dante's poetic friends. Dante's putative subject is Beatrice/Love—but the *Vita Nuova* is really an exercise in poetry: Dante sets the emotional scene for a poem, then he writes the poem, then he explains the poem's structure, part by part. Dante himself later became uncomfortable with this work of youth, but he did not disown it.

This selected edition of *Dante and His Circle* concentrates on the eternal theme of Love, leaving aside poems relating to the wars and politics of the time. Love as a subject of serious public discussion signaled the emerging Renaissance, not just a rediscovery of the glories of ancient Greece and Rome, but a new sensibility finding—no—building a platform for personal expression and interchange.

Besides the *Vita Nuova*, Rossetti arranged some poetic exchanges between Dante and *Guido Cavalcanti*. Guido was fifteen years older than Dante, the scion of a very old noble family of Florence, a leader of the White faction, a Guelf. Both he and Dante had been students of Brunetto Latini, possibly at the same time. Guido was an agnostic, as his father had been, though he is reported to have gone on at least one pilgrimage. Full of self-reliant pride, he excelled in every sport and was a natural leader. Rash, fickle, presumptuous, Guido was also tall and handsome. By a political marriage to a Ghibelline woman, Beatrice Uberti, daughter of Farinata Uberti, Cavalcanti secured for himself the leadership of the Ghibelline faction. Soon afterward, internal strife forced the Ghibellines into exile from Florence. Guido also had a personal feud with Corso Donati, leader of one of the Guelf factions. Pope Boniface VIII attempted to calm the Florentine atmosphere, but his emissary was sent packing with no results.

In 1301, Dante and other civic leaders banished leaders of both the White and Black parties, including Guido Cavalcanti. Shortly afterward, Guido contracted a disease and died. And shortly after that, while Dante was out of the city on a trip to Rome, he himself was declared to be exiled for showing too much favor to the White Party. Through all the succeeding fluctuations of Florentine politics, Florence was never able to entice him back.

In the circle of poets, *Cino da Pistoia* was Dante's "second" friend—their boyhood companionship developed into a correspondence and lifelong friendship. Cino is "amicus ejus" (his friend) and "frater carissime" (dear brother) to Dante.

Cino was born Guittoncino de' Sinibuldi in Pistoia, twenty miles from Florence, in 1270, five years after Dante's birth. He became a lawyer and public servant—by 1307 he is Florence's Assessor of Civil Causes. But the turmoil between the Whites and the Blacks forced Cino to leave for Lombardy, where he met and fell in love with the lady Selvaggia Vergiolesi. Unfortunately, the weak White faction was forced to retreat further into the mountains, where Selvaggia died of illness at Monte della Sambuca. Cino then journeyed to France, Tuscany, and finally Rome, where at last he secured an appointment. He was enlisted by Louis of Savoy to help prepare matters for Henry of Luxembourg's arrival in Rome for his coronation as Henry VII, Emperor of the Holy Roman Empire. Henry was sympathetic to the White Party (Ghibellines) and his rise to power created hopes for a political turnaround. Three years later Henry was poisoned.

In these charged circumstances, Cino returned to Pistoia and served again in public office. He now married Margherita deglis Ughi and had five children. His only son, Minu, helped the Ghibellines retake power in Pistoia, but this era lasted less than three years.

Throughout his life, Cino wrote poetry, and when his situation settled down, he taught at several of the newly founded Italian universities. Petrarch was probably a student of his. When Cino da Pistoia died at age 66, he was a prosperous man.

The other figures in Dante's "circle" are known mainly for their poetry; the events of their lives, in some cases, are entirely unknown.

Dante da Maiano (Dante is short for Durante) loved a Sicilian woman named Nina. His rhymes are coarse, his subjects crude. Nothing else of his life is known.

Cecco Angiolieri of Siena earned a place in Dante's *Divine Comedy*. He was a scamp whose main passion in poetry was hatred of his father. He loved Becchina, a lady who was already married; when Dante scolded him for this affair, Cecco turned on him. Cecco was handsome and well-bred, but when a gambler tricked him out of his money and his new clothes, he was ashamed to go home. This episode set Cecco on a course of self-destruction. His poetry, close to natural speech, was frequently impious or licentious. Dante knew him early in his life, but in later life avoided his company.

Guido Orlandi, as you will see in his poetry, is a bore, a complainer, a critic.

About *Bernardo da Bologna* nothing is known.

Gianni Alfani was Florentine, of a noble family.

Dino Compagni, born around 1259, wrote a chronicle of Florence. He was of noble blood, and held public office. He died two years after Dante did, in 1323.

Lapo Gianni fell out of favor with the group at some point. He was a friend of Guido, and he may have been a cousin of Dante's. He was a notary.

Dino Frescobaldi once was said to have saved the first draft of Dante's *Inferno* from pillage.

Giotto di Bondone, the great painter, was an intimate of Dante's. He was twelve years younger, born in 1276 at Vespignano, 14 miles from Florence. Dante watched Giotto at work at Padua, and Giotto visited Dante at his last residence in exile in Ravenna. One source says that Dante had studied drawing with Giotto's master Cimabue—and Dante describes himself in the *Vita Nuova* as being so absorbed in a drawing that he is unconscious of onlookers. A painting of the young Dante by Giotto can be seen in the Bargello, at the chapel of the Podesta.

Of *Simone dall' Antella*, nothing is known.

Giovanni Quirino is probably a Venetian bishop who knew the older Dante through correspondence.

Forese Donati was the brother of Dante's wife Gemma, and also the brother of Corso Donati, Guido Cavalcanti's nemesis. Dante and Forese were youths together in some disorderly escapades. The friendship did not flourish, but Dante wept at Forese's death. Forese wrote bad poetry.

Giovanni Boccaccio is included by Rossetti in an appendix, since Boccaccio was only seven years old when Dante died. His poems of homage reveal the esteem that Italians to this day show toward Dante.

I have also included *Guido Guinicelli* in this book; even though he and Dante are not known to have met, the teenage Dante emulated Guinicelli's love poetry.

Onesto di Boncima is included because Cino chides Dante for not including his friend in the *Commedia*—and in the spirit of poetic exchange *Terino da Castel Fiorentino* answers a sonnet of Onesto's. All three of these poets were translated by Rossetti, and grouped in his *Early Italian Poets*, preceding the publication of the *Circle*.

Little is known of Dante's own childhood or adolescence, but by the age of eighteen, he was already writing philosophical love poetry. His acknowledged mentors were Guido Guinicelli of Bologna, whom he mentions in his *Commedia*, Guido Cavalcanti, his friend fifteen years older than himself, and Brunetto Latini, one of the leaders of Florentine politics. Dante was intimate with the painter Giotto, the musician Casella, and he early interested himself in public service.

Altogether, the group around Dante is quite varied. Many were mutual acquaintances from an early age, not surprising in a city as small as Florence. The tumultuous factionalism between Guelfs and Ghibellines reflected fractious shifts in power between the feudal countryside, mercantile town, papacy, empire, nobility, and populist aspirations—battles and mass exiles had been going on in Florence since the time of Countess Matilda in 1054 and continued through the reign of the Medici in the sixteenth century. Dante and his friends lived in interesting times.

What did Dante Gabriel Rossetti see in this motley collection of Italian poets of the early Renaissance? Their impact was undeniable in the rise of European national literatures, sounding themes that young poets today still aspire to capture—love, freedom, personal values. Were they backward-looking, searching in the rubble of Rome and Greece for models, as the founders of Renaissance architecture, art and literature did? Or had they breathed new air from the East and Islamic Spain, amalgamating the best of several cultures into a new sensibility?

Rossetti saw their accomplishment as a fresh start. Dante and the poets around him forged a new beginning in European letters. Rejecting the Medieval Latin tradition as well as the Latin language, this band of friends around Dante experimented with new forms of poetry learned from Provençal troubadour poets and their jongleur musicians, and accepted the doctrine of courtly love.

Dante elaborates in another book his choice of language—Latin was universal but lacked the nuances he was interested in. Provençal, the language of the Troubadours, had the sophistication and concepts, but was not immediately accessible to his audience. No, he would write poetry as the people around him actually spoke; he would, with his friends, legitimize the fluid poetic romance language we know as Italian. He and the others abandoned Latin meter in favor of end-line rhyme. In fact, the works of Dante are still used as a standard for cultured Italian language; in much the same way, the Elizabethan writers in England regularized and popularized the London dialect to create modern English. Thus a national literature was born among Dante and his friends, to become a cornerstone of modern European culture.

Dante's treatment of love deserves special comment. Sir Kenneth Clark says that courtly love, the chivalrous code of a man's submission to an unapproachable woman "was entirely unknown to antiquity ... this would have seemed to the Romans or to the Vikings not only absurd but unbelievable." Where did such an idea come from? Dante's ideal of love appears to owe no more than a patina of holiness to mariolatry, worship of the mother of Jesus. The short answer is Provence; Dante knew the work of the Provençal poets Arnaut Daniel, Bertran de Born, Giraut de Bornelh, Folquet of Marseilles and the Italian troubadour Sordello well enough to include them in his *Commedia*. These were only a few of the four hundred known troubadours, who spread the ideal of courtly love. The most remarkable fact about the new forms and themes of this Provençal poetry is that they owed little or nothing to Latin poetry.

The particular form of Provençal courtly love as practiced at the court of Eleanor of Aquitaine, William IX's granddaughter, had several sources. First of all, during the Crusades, when the lord of the manor was absent, the lady of the court held real power, but was also married and unavailable. Second, contacts with the Muslim world and other foreign influences in the Levant opened new horizons to the Crusaders and their soldiers. And third, since most noble marriages were arranged between families, a courtly game of love and romance might be permitted the young women once they were safely married. Thus the ladies of the court welcomed the troubadours—who always sang of unapproachable ladies in their songs.

Also current in Provence was a widespread religious sect known as the Albigensians. They experimented with communal living, free love, ecstatic spiritual experiences, and a rejection of the authority of the Roman Catholic Church. Whole sections of the country were swept up by these ideas, and the Papacy decided on a drastic course of action—heretic hunting.

The campaign against the Albigensian heresy was so successful that it wrecked the economy of southern France. Wholesale slaughter of the unrepentant, burning of towns, and rigid moral laws broke the back of the revolt. So thorough was the expunging of the Albigensians from southern France that we have very little documentation on their ideas, except that they were anathema to the Roman Church. Any troubadours still alive fled to Spain and northern Italy, including Florence. Thus it was that Provence influenced Dante and his friends.

The question remains, where did these ideas come from? Some forms of Provençal poetry worked particularly well for court situations of polite mixed audience, such as the *sirventes* (social satire), *ballada* (song with long refrain), *planh* (dirge), and *tenson* (dialogue on love, religion, or a satire). Other forms were more personal—the *pastourella* (pastorale), *alba* (morning song), and *serena* (evening song). These latter probably developed directly from Mozarabic, a mixed language spoken by Christians in Arab-dominated Spain. There, love poetry was flourishing. The *muwassaha* ("girdled") form employed verse and refrain with end rhymes and internal rhymes, and was used for the poetry of love.

Around 900 A.D., a blind poet named Mocadem, who lived near Cordoba, wrote Mozarabic personal poems in the forms of *markas*, *zajals*, and *muwassahas*. This new erotic poetry broke with convention to introduce the idea of expressing one's emotions publicly, celebrating the self. Other Western Arab poets who explored this new vein of self-expression included Ibn

Hamdis of Sicily, Ibn Rashiq of Qayrawan, Ibn Zaydun of Cordoba, Mu'tamid, king of Seville, and Ibn Ammar. Ibn Quzman, a troubadour, excelled in the *zajal* form.

In 1085, Toledo was captured by the Christians, but remained a center of translation of Arab and Persian classics, including Firdausi (b. 941); his *Yusuf-u-Zulaikha* (Joseph and Zuleika), is a thoroughly romantic epic. By 1100 A.D., many *markas* were written in Romance language, and transliterated into Hebrew and Arabic *muwassahas*. Thus the ideas of the East came to Dante from the West, and to Provence from further West—Arabic Spain.

Dante Gabriel Rossetti was, in a sense, born to create this book. His father, Gabriele Rossetti, an Italian political refugee in England, was a lecturer in Italian literature, a Dante expert known for his original but eccentric ideas. D.G.'s mother was a sister of Dr. John Polidori, Byron's literary doctor friend, who was present when Mary Shelley invented the *Frankenstein* story. D.G.'s sister, Christina, earned her own reputation as a poet, as did his brother William.

The Pre-Raphaelite Brotherhood in Victorian England was D.G.'s idea of reviving or bringing to life the excitement of a close circle of talented friends changing the course of Europe's intellectual progress—as happened at the court of Eleanor of Aquitaine, in Provence, and in Florence. Rossetti himself produced a few pieces of art true to the ideas espoused, although the thrust of the movement was clearer in its conception than in its achievements.

Rossetti and his circle—Millais, Holman Hunt, his brother William, Burne-Jones, William Morris, with support by John Ruskin—shared an intellectual adventure much like Dante's circumstances. The activities of this group of friends no doubt suggested to Rossetti the unique structure of "Dante and His Circle."

I have re-arranged the poems to emphasize interchanges that may or may not have taken place between the poets. Dante's *Vita Nuova* is presented intact, yet in the context of a flow of ideas. The marginalia are Dante's own comments on his poems, making this one of the most introspective pieces of literature ever written.

Poems of Rossetti's anthology that did not bear on the theme of love have not been included in this selection. Where possible, Rossetti's language has been shorn of Victorianisms that jar on the modern sensibility. A glossary is provided for terms that are no longer in current usage.

Although it may seem to many feminists today that idealization of the woman as a figure of romantic love is retrograde, this conception was a giant step forward in human development at the time. Though no female poets are represented in this grouping, the poems make it clear that women were neither helpless nor servile in Florentine society.

One characteristic that deserves a special note, is the personification of Death, Love, and other abstract concepts. In the middle of the *Vita Nuova*, Dante specifically sets forth the doctrine of "poetic license," the claim that a poet is entitled to employ metaphor, and, in particular, anthropomorphizing, in order to talk about certain subjects, such as beseeching Death on behalf of one's beloved. This new technique allowed, or perhaps introduced, broad possibilities of projecting inner dialogue or personal psychology in a public way. In poetry and in art, as with Giotto, the foundations of the Renaissance were emerging for a greater appreciation of the individual.

As late as the Nineteenth Century, the poet Percy Bysshe Shelley felt it necessary to invoke Dante's doctrine of poetic license, in order to claim the same license for written prose. He states this explicitly in the preface to his wife's (Mary Shelley), speculative fiction novel, *Frankenstein*, a tale that goes beyond the plausible in order to explore ideas that might never be reached with reality-based prose.

Sasha Newborn
October 2012

Love and the Ladies

Lappo's Lady

LAPPO GIANNI

Madrigal: What Love shall provide for him

Love, I demand to have my lady in fee.

        Fine balm let Arno be;
the walls of Florence all of silver reared,
and crystal pavements in the public way.

        With castles make me feared,
till every Latin soul have owned my sway.

Be the world peaceful; safe throughout each path;
        no neighbor to breed wrath;
the air, summer and winter, temperate.

A thousand dames and damsels richly clad
        upon my choice to wait,
singing by day and night to make me glad.

Let me have fruitful gardens of great girth,
        filled with the strife of birds,
with water-springs, and beasts that house in the earth.

Let me seem Solomon for lore of words,
Samson for strength, for beauty Absalom.

        Knights as my serfs be given;
and as I will, let music go and come;
till at the last you bring me into Heaven.

Guido Cavalcanti

Sonnet to Dante Alighieri: *He reports, in a feigned vision, the successful issue of Lapo Gianni's love*

Dante, a sigh that rose from the heart's core
    assailed me, while I slumbered, suddenly:
so that I woke on the instant, fearing sore
    lest it came there in Love's company:
till, turning, I beheld the servitor
    of Lady Lagia: "Help me," so said he,
"O help me, Pity." Though he said no more,
    so much of Pity's essence entered me,
that I was ware of Love, those shafts he wields
    a-whetting, and preferred the mourner's quest
    to him, who straightway answered on this wise:
"Go tell my servant that the lady yields,
    and that I hold her now at his behest:
        if he believe not, let him note her eyes."

Dante Alighieri

Sonnet to Guido Cavalcanti: He imagines a pleasant voyage for Guido, Lapo Gianni, and himself, with their three ladies

Guido, I wish that Lappo, you, and I,
    could be by spells conveyed, as it were now,
    upon a barque, with all the winds that blow
across all seas at our good will to hie.
So no mischance nor temper of the sky
    should mar our course with spite or cruel slip;
    but we, observing old companionship,
to be companions still should long thereby.
And Lady Joan, and Lady Beatrice,
    and her the thirtieth on my roll, with us
        should our good wizard set, over seas to move
        and not to talk of anything but love:
and they three ever to be well at ease,
    as we should be, I think, if this were thus.

GUIDO CAVALCANTI

Sonnet to Dante Alighieri: Guido answers the foregoing sonnet, speaking with shame of his changed love

If I were still that man, worthy to love,
   of whom I have but the remembrance now,
   or if the lady bore another brow,
to hear this thing might bring me joy thereof.
But you, who in Love's proper court do move,
   even there where hope is born of grace—see how
   my very soul within me is brought low:
for a swift archer, whom his feats approve,
   now bends the bow, which Love to him did yield,
     in such mere sport against me, it would seem
     as though he held his lordship for a jest.
     Then hear the marvel which is sorriest—
   my sorely wounded soul forgives him,
yet knows that in his act her strength is killed.

GUIDO CAVALCANTI

Sonnet to Dante Alighieri: He mistrusts the love of Lapo Gianni

I pray you, Dante, should you meet with Love
   in any place where Lappo then may be,
   that there you fail not to mark heedfully
if Love with lover's name that man approve;
if to our Master's will his lady move
   aright, and if himself show fealty:
   for ofttimes, by ill custom, you may see
this sort profess the semblance of true love.
You know that in the court where Love holds sway
   a law subsists, that no man who is vile
     can service yield to a lost woman there.
     If suffering aught avail the sufferer,
   you straightway shall discern our lofty style
which needs the badge of honor must display.

Lappo Gianni

Ballata: A message in charge for his lady Lagia

Ballad, since Love himself has fashioned you
   within my mind where he does make abode,
     hie you to her who through my eyes bestowed
her blessing on my heart, which stays with me.

Since you were born a handmaiden of Love,
   with every grace you should be perfected,
     and everywhere seem gentle, wise, and sweet.
And for that your aspect gives sign thereof,
   I do not tell you, "Thus much must be said"—
     hoping, if you inherit my wit,
     and come on her when speech may ill befit,
that you will say no words of any kind:
but when her ear is graciously inclined,
   address her without dread submissively.
Afterward, when your courteous speech is done,
   (ended with fair obeisance and salute
     to that chief forehead of serenest good)
wait you the answer which, in heavenly tone,
   shall haply stir between her lips, nigh mute
     for gentleness and virtuous womanhood.
     And mark that, if my homage please her mood,
no rose shall be incarnate in her cheek,
but her soft eyes shall seem subdued and meek,
   and almost pale her face for delicacy.
For, when at last your amorous discourse
   shall have possessed her spirit with that fear
     of thoughtful recollection which in love
comes first—then say you that my heart implores
   only without an end to honor her,
     till by God's will my living soul remove:
     that I take counsel oftentimes with Love;
for he first made my hope thus strong and rife,
through whom my heart, my mind, and all my life,
   are given in bondage to her seigniory.
Then shall you find the blessed refuge girt
   in the circle of her arms, where pity and grace
     have sojourn, with all human excellence:
then shall you feel her gentleness exert

       its rule (unless, alack! she deem you base):
          then shall you know her sweet intelligence:
          then shall you see—O marvel most intense!—
what thing the beauty of the angels is,
and what are the miraculous harmonies
      whereon Love rears the heights of sovereignty.
Move, Ballad, so that none take note of you,
      until you set your footsteps in Love's road.
      Having arrived, speak with your visage bowed,
and bring no false doubt back, or jealousy.

GUIDO CAVALCANTI

Sonnet: On the detection of a false friend

Love and the lady Lagia, Guido and I,
      unto a certain lord are bounden all,
      who has released us—know you from whose thrall?
Yet I'll not speak, but let the matter die:
since now these three no more are held thereby,
      who in such homage at his feet did fall
      that I myself was not more whimsical,
in him conceiving godship from on high.
Let Love be thanked the first, who first discerned
      the truth; and that wise lady afterward,
          who in fit time took back her heart again;
and Guido next, from worship wholly turned;
      and I, as he. But if you have not heard,
          I shall not tell how much I loved him then.

Cecco's Lady

CECCO ANGIOLIERI

Sonnet: Of Becchina, the shoemaker's daughter

Why, if Becchina's heart were diamond,
    and all the other parts of her were steel,
    as cold to love as snows when they congeal
in lands to which the sun may not get round;
and if her father were a giant crowned
    and not a donkey born to stitching shoes,
    or I were but an ass myself—to use
such harshness, scarce could to her praise redound.
Yet if she'd only for a minute hear,
    and I could speak if only pretty well,
        I'd let her know that I'm her happiness;
that I'm her life should also be made clear,
    with other things that I've no need to tell;
        and then I feel quite sure she'd answer "Yes."

CECCO ANGIOLIERI

Sonnet: Of Becchina, and of her husband

I would like better in the grace to be
    of the dear mistress whom I bear in mind
    (as once I was) than I should like to find
a stream that washed up gold continually:
because no language could report of me
    the joys that round my heart would then be twined,
    who now, without her love, do seem resigned
to death that bends my life to its decree.
And one thing makes the matter still more sad:
    for all the while I know the fault's my own,
    that on her husband I take no revenge,
who's worse to her than is to me my dad.
    God send grief has not pulled my courage down,
    that hearing this I laugh; for it seems strange.

CECCO ANGIOLIERI

Sonnet: In absence from Becchina

My heart's so heavy with a hundred things
    that I fell dead a hundred times a day;
yet death would be the least of sufferings,
    for life's all suffering save what's slept away;
though even in sleep there is no dream but brings
    from dream-land such dull torture as it may.
And yet one moment would pluck out these stings,
    if for one moment she were mine today
who gives my heart the anguish that it has.
    Each thought that seeks my heart for its abode
    becomes a wan and sorrow-stricken guest:
sorrow has brought me to so sad a pass
    that men look sad to meet me on the road;
    nor any road is mine that leads to rest.

Guido Cavalcanti

Sonnet to Cecco Angiolieri: *To a newly enriched man; reminding him of the wants of the poor*

As you were loathe to see, before your feet,
   the dear broad coin roll all your hill-slope down,
   till, 'twixt the cracks of the hard glebe, some clown
should find, rub oft, and scarcely render it—
tell me, I charge you, if by generous heat
   or clutching frost the fruits of earth be grown,
   and by what wind the blight is over them strown,
and with what gloom the tempest is replete.
Moreover (an' it please you), when at morn
   you hear the voice of the poor husbander,
     and those loud herds, his other family—
I feel quite sure that if Becchina's born
   with a kind heart, she does the best she can
     to wheedle some of your new wealth from you.

Cecco Angiolieri

Sonnet: *He rails against Dante, who had censured his homage to Becchina*

Dante Alighieri in Becchina's praise
   won't have me sing, and bears him like my lord.
   He's but a pinchbeck florin, on my word;
sugar he seems, but salt's in all his ways;
he looks like wheaten bread, who's bread of maize;
   he's but a sty, though like a tower in height;
   a falcon, till you find that he's a kite;
call him a cock!—a hen's more like his case.
Go not to Florence, sonnet of my own,
   and there with dames and maids hold pretty parleys,
     and say that all he is does only seem.
And I meanwhile will make him better known
   unto the Count of Provence, good King Charles;
     and in this way we'll singe his skin for him.

CECCO ANGIOLIERI

Sonnet: Of Love, in honor of his mistress Becchina

Whatever good is naturally done
    is born of Love as fruit is born of flower:
    by Love all good is brought to its full power:
yea, Love does more than this; for he finds none
so coarse but from his touch some grace is won,
    and the poor wretch is altered in an hour.
    So let it be decreed that Death devour
the beast who says that Love's a thing to shun.
A man's just worth the good that he can hold,
    and where no love is found, no good is there;
        on that there's nothing that I would not stake.
So now, my sonnet, go as you are told
    to lovers and their sweethearts everywhere,
        and say I made you for Becchina's sake.

CECCO ANGIOLIERI

Sonnet: Of the 20th June 1291

I'm full of everything I do not want,
    and have not that wherein I should find ease;
    for alway till Becchina brings me peace
the heavy heart I bear must toil and pant;
that so all written paper would prove scant
    (though in its space the Bible you might squeeze)
    to say how like the flames of furnaces
I burn, remembering what she used to grant.
Because the stars are fewer in heaven's span
    than all those kisses wherewith I kept tune
        all in an instant (I who now have none!)
upon her mouth (I and no other man!)
    so sweetly on the twentieth day of June
        in the new year twelve hundred ninety-one.

Cavalcanti and Various Ladies

GUIDO CAVALCANTI

Sonnet: *He compares all things with his lady, and finds them wanting*

Beauty in women; the high will's decree;
   fair knighthood armed for manly exercise;
   the pleasant song of birds; love's soft replies;
the strength of rapid ships upon the sea;
the serene air when light begins to be;
   the white snow, without wind that falls and lies;
   fields of all flower; the place where waters rise;
silver and gold; azure in jewellery—
weighed against these, the sweet and quiet worth
   which my dear lady cherishes at heart
     might seem a little matter to be shown;
   being truly, over these, as much apart
as the whole heaven is greater than this earth.
     All good to kindred natures cleaves soon.

GUIDO CAVALCANTI
Ballata: Of his lady among other ladies

With other women I beheld my love—
    not that the rest were women to my eyes,
who only as her shadows seemed to move.

I do not praise her more than with the truth,
    nor blame I these if it be rightly read.

But while I speak, a thought I may not soothe
    says to my senses: "Soon shall you be dead,
    if for my sake your tears you will not shed."

And then the eyes yield passage, at that thought,
to the heart's weeping, which forgets her not.

GUIDO CAVALCANTI
Sonnet: To his lady Joan, of Florence

Flowers have you in yourself, and foliage,
    and what is good, and what is glad to see;
the sun is not so bright as your visage;
    all is stark naught when one has looked on you;
there is not such a beautiful personage
    anywhere on the green earth verily;
if one fear love, your bearing sweet and sage
    comforts him, and no more fear has he.
Your lady friends and maidens ministering
    are all, for love of you, much to my taste:
and much I pray them that in everything
    they honor you even as you meritest,
and have you in their gentle harboring:
    because among them all you are the best.

GUIDO CAVALCANTI

Sonnet: A rapture concerning his lady

Who is she coming, whom all gaze upon,
    who makes the air all tremulous with light,
and at whose side is Love himself? that none
    dare speak, but each man's sighs are infinite.
    Ah me! how she looks round from left to right,
let Love discourse: I may not speak thereon.
Lady she seems of such high benison
    as makes all others graceless in men's sight.
The honor which is hers cannot be said;
    to whom are subject all things virtuous,
        while all things beauteous own her deity.
Never was the mind of man so nobly led,m
    nor yet was such redemption granted us
        that we should ever know her perfectly.

GUIDO CAVALCANTI

Sonnet: Of the eyes of a certain Mandetta, of Toulouse, which resemble those of his lady Joan, of Florence

A certain youthful lady in Toulouse,
    gentle and fair, of cheerful modesty,
    is in her eyes, with such exact degree,
of likeness unto my own lady, whose
I am, that through the heart she does abuse
    the soul to sweet desire. It goes from me
    to her; yet, fearing, says not who is she
that of a truth its essence thus subdues.
This lady looks on it with the sweet eyes
    whose glance did erst the wounds of Love anoint.
        through its true lady's eyes which are as they.
Then to the heart returns it, full of sighs,
    wounded to death by a sharp arrow's point
        wherewith this lady speeds it on its way.

GUIDO CAVALCANTI

Ballata: He reveals, in a dialogue, his increasing love for Mandetta

Being in thought of love, I chanced to see
    two youthful damozels.
  One sang: "Our life inhales
    all love continually."

Their aspect was so utterly serene,
    so courteous, of such quiet nobleness,
that I said to them: "Yours, I may well ween,
    'tis of all virtue to unlock the place.
    Ah! damozels, do not account him base
      whom thus his wound subdues:
      since I was at Toulouse,
        my heart is dead in me."

They turned their eyes upon me in so much
    as to perceive how wounded was my heart;
while, of the spirits born of tears, one such
    had been begotten through the constant smart.
    Then seeing me, abashed, to turn apart,
      one of them said, and laughed:
      "Love, look you, by his craft
        holds this man thoroughly."

But with grave sweetness, after a brief while,
    she who at first had laughed on me replied,
saying: "This lady, who by Love's great guile
    her countenance in your heart has glorified,
    looked you so deep within the eyes, Love sighed
      and was awakened there.
      If it seem ill to bear,
        in him your hope must be."

The second piteous maiden, of all ruth,
    fashioned for sport in Love's own image, said:
"This stroke, whereof your heart bears trace in sooth,
    from eyes of too much puissance was shed,
    whence in your heart such brightness entered,
      you may not look thereon.

>   Say, of those eyes that shone
>   can you remember you?"

Then said I, yielding answer therewithal
        unto this virgin's difficult behest:
"A lady of Toulouse, whom Love does call
        Mandetta, sweetly kirtled and enlaced,
        I do remember to my sore unrest.
            Yea, by her eyes indeed
            my life has been decreed
                to death inevitably."

Go, ballad, to the city, even Toulouse,
        and softly entering the Daurade, look round
        and softly call that so there may be found
some lady who for complaisance may choose
to show you her who can my life confuse.
    And if she yield you way,
    lift you your voice and say:
        "For grace I come to you."

Gianni Alfani

Sonnet to Guido Cavalcanti: On the part of a lady of Pisa

Guido, that Gianni who, a day agone,
    sought you, now greets you (ay and you may laugh!)
    on that same Pisan beauty's sweet behalf
who can deal love-wounds even as you have done.
She asked me whether your good will were prone
    for service unto Love who troubles her,
    if she to you in suchwise should repair
that, save by him and Gualtier, 'twere not known—
for thus her kindred of ill augury
    should lack the means wherefrom there might be planned
        worse harm than lying speech that smites afar.
I told her that you have continually
    a goodly sheaf of arrows to your hand,
        which well should stead her in such gentle war.

Bernardo da Bologna

Sonnet to Guido Cavalcanti: He writes to Guido, telling him of the love which a certain Pinella showed on seeing him

    Unto that lowly lovely maid, I wis,
        so poignant in the heart was your salute,
        that she changed countenance, remaining mute.
Wherefore I asked: "Pinella, how is this?
has heard of Guido? know you who he is?"
    She answered, "Yea"; then paused, irresolute;
    but I saw well how the love-wounds acute
were widened, and the star which Love calls his
filled her with gentle brightness perfectly.
    "But, friend, an't please you, I would have it told,"
she said, "how I am known to him through you.
    Yet since, scarce seen, I knew his name of old—
even as the riddle is read, so must it be.
    Oh! send him love of mine a thousand-fold!"

Guido Cavalcanti

Sonnet to Bernardo da Bologna: Guido answers, commending Pinella, and saying that the love he can offer her is already shared by many noble ladies

The fountainhead that is so bright to see
    gains as it runs in virtue and in sheen,
friend Bernard; and for her who spoke with you,
    even such the flow of her young life has been:
so that when Love discourses secretly
    of things the fairest he has ever seen,
he says there is no fairer thing than she,
    a lowly maid as lovely as a queen.
And for that I am troubled, thinking of
    that sigh wherein I burn upon the waves
        which drift her heart—poor barque, so ill bested!
unto Pinella a great river of love
    I send, that's full of sirens, and whose slaves
        are beautiful and richly habited.

Guido Cavalcanti

Ballata: Concerning a shepherd maid

Within a copse I met a shepherd maid,
more fair, I said, than any star to see.
She came with waving tresses pale and bright,
    with rosy cheer, and loving eyes of flame,
guiding the lambs beneath her wand aright.
    Her naked feet still had the dews on them,
    as, singing like a lover, so she came;
joyful, and fashioned for all ecstasy.

I greeted her at once, and question made
    what escort had she through the woods in spring?
But with soft accents she replied and said
    that she was all alone there, wandering:
        moreover: "Do you know, when the birds sing,
my heart's desire is for a mate," said she.

While she was telling me this wish of hers,
    the birds were all in song throughout the wood.
"Even now then," said my thought, "the time recurs,
    with my own longing to assuage her mood."
    And so, in her sweet favor's name, I sued
that she would kiss there and embrace with me.

She took my hand to her with amorous will,
    and answered that she gave me all her heart,
and drew me where the leaf is fresh and still,
    where spring the woodflowers in the shade apart.
    And on that day, by Joy's enchanted art,
there Love in very presence seemed to be.

GUIDO CAVALCANTI

Sonnet: Of his pain from a new love

Why from the danger did my eyes not start—
    why not become even blind—ere through my sight
    within my soul you ever could alight
to say: "Do you not hear me in your heart?"
New torment then, the old torment's counterpart,
    filled me at once with such a sore affright,
    that, Lady, lady (I said), destroy not quite
my eyes and me! O help us where you art!
You have so left my eyes, that Love is fain—
    even Love himself—with pity uncontrolled
        to bend above them, weeping for their loss:
saying: "If any man feel heavy pain,
    this man's more painful heart let him behold:
        Death has it in her hand, cut like a cross."

Guido Orlandi

Prolonged Sonnet: He finds fault with the conceits of the foregoing sonnet

Friend, well I know you know well to bear
    your sword's-point, that it pierce the close-locked mail:
    and like a bird to flit from perch to pale:
and out of difficult ways to find the air:
largely to take and generously to share:
    thrice to secure advantage: to regale
    greatly the great, and over lands prevail.
In all you are, one only fault is there:
for still among the wise of wit you say
    that Love himself does weep for your estate;
        and yet, no eyes no tears: lo now, your whim!
Soft, rather say: This is not held in haste;
    but bitter are the hours and passionate,
        to him that loves, and love is not for him.
For me (by usage strengthened to forbear
from carnal love), I fall not in such snare.

Dino Compagni

Sonnet to Guido Cavalcanti: He reproves Guido for his arrogance in love

No man may mount upon a golden stair,
   Guido my master, to Love's palace-sill:
no key of gold will fit the lock that's there,
   nor heart there enter without pure goodwill.
Not if he miss one courteous duty, dare
   a lover hope he should his love fulfill;
but to his lady must make meek repair,
   reaping with husbandry her favors still.
And you but know of Love (I think) his name:
   youth holds your reason in extremities:
   only on your own face you turn your eyes;
fairer than Absalom's accounted the same;
and think, as rosy moths are drawn by flame,
   to draw the women from their balconies.

Guido Cavalcanti

Sonnet: He speaks of a third love of his

O you that often have within your eyes
   a Love who holds three shafts—know you from me
   that this my sonnet would commend to you
(come from afar) a soul in heavy sighs,
which even by Love's sharp arrow wounded lies.
   Twice did the Syrian archer shoot, and he
   now bends his bow the third time, cunningly,
that, you being here, he wound me in no wise.
Because the soul would quicken at the core
   thereby, which now is near to utter death,
      from these two shafts, a triple wound that yield.
   The first gives pleasure, yet disquiets;
and with the second is the longing for
      the mighty gladness by the third fulfilled.

Guido Cavalcanti
Sonnet: Of an ill-favored lady

Just look, Manetto, at that wry-mouthed minx;
   merely take notice what a wretch it is;
   how well contrived in her deformities,
how beastly favored when she scowls and blinks.
Why, with a hood on (if one only thinks)
   or muffle of prim veils and scapularies—
   and set together, on a day like this,
some pretty lady with the odious sphinx—
why, then your sins could hardly have such weight,
   nor you be so subdued from Love's attack,
      nor so possessed in Melancholy's sway,
but that perforce your peril must be great
   of laughing till the very heartstrings crack:
      either you'd die, or you must run away.

Guido Cavalcanti
Sonnet: To a friend who does not pity his love

If I entreat this lady that all grace
   seem not unto her heart an enemy,
   foolish and evil you declare me,
and desperate in idle stubbornness.
Whence is such cruel judgment yours, whose face,
   to him that looks thereon, professes you
   faithful, and wise, and of all courtesy,
and made after the way of gentleness?
Alas! my soul within my heart does find
   sighs, and its grief by weeping does enhance,
      that, drowned in bitter tears, those sighs depart:
and then there seems a presence in the mind,
   as of a lady's thoughtful countenance
      come to behold the death of the poor heart.

Guido Cavalcanti
Ballata: Of a continual death in love

Though you, indeed, have quite forgotten ruth,
its steadfast truth my heart abandons not;
but still its thought yields service in good part
        to that hard heart in you.

Alas! who hears believes not I am so.
Yet who can know? of very surety, none.
From love is won a spirit, in some wise,
        which dies perpetually:

and, when at length in that strange ecstasy
        the heavy sigh will start,
        there rains upon my heart
        a love so pure and fine,
that I say, "Lady, I am wholly yours."

An Assortment of Ladies

GUIDO GUINICELLI
Sonnet: *He will praise his lady*

Yea, let me praise my lady whom I love:
    likening her unto the lily and rose:
    brighter than morning star her visage glows;
she is beneath even as her Saint above;
she is as the air in summer which God wove
    of purple and of vermilion glorious;
    as gold and jewels richer than man knows.
Love's self, being love for her, must holier prove.
Ever as she walks she has a sober grace,
    making bold men abashed and good men glad;
        if she delight you not, your heart must err.
No man dare look on her, his thoughts being base:
    Nay, let me say even more than I have said—
no man could think base thoughts who looked on her.

Dante Alighieri

Ballata: He will gaze upon Beatrice

Because my eyes can never had their fill
  of looking at my lady's lovely face,
    I will so fix my gaze
that I may become blessed, beholding her.
Even as an angel, up at his great height
standing amid the light,
    becomes blessed by only seeing God—
So, though I be a simple earthly wight,
yet nonetheless I might,
    beholding her who is my heart's dear load,
    be blessed, and in the spirit soar abroad.
Such power abides in that gracious one;
albeit felt of none
    save of him who, desiring, honors her.

Guido Cavalcanti

Sonnet to Guido Orlandi: In praise of Guido Orlandi's lady

A lady in whom love is manifest—
  that love which perfect honor does adorn—
has taken the living heart out of your breast,
  which in her keeping to new life is born:
for there by such sweet power it is possessed
  as even is felt of Indian unicorn:
and all its virtue now, with fierce unrest,
  unto your soul makes difficult return.
For this your lady is virtue's minister
  in suchwise that no fault there is to show,
    save that God made her mortal on this ground.
    and even herein His wisdom shall be found:
  for only thus our intellect could know
that heavenly beauty which resembles her.

Guido Orlandi

Sonnet to Guido Cavalcanti: *He answers the foregoing sonnet, declaring himself his lady's champion*

To sound of trumpet rather than of horn,
   I in Love's name would hold a battle-play
   of gentlemen in arms on Easter Day;
and, sailing without oar or wind, be borne
unto my joyful beauty; all that morn
   to ride round her, in her cause seeking fray
   of arms with all but you, friend, who does say
the truth of her, and whom all truths adorn.
And still I pray Our Lady's grace above,
   most reverently, that she whom my thoughts bear
     in sweet remembrance own her Lord supreme.
Holding her honor dear, as does behove—
   in God who therewithal sustains her
     let her abide, and not depart from Him.

Onesto di Boncima

Sonnet: *He wishes that he could meet his lady alone*

Whether all grace have failed I scarce may scan,
   be it of mere mischance, or art's ill sway,
   that this wise, Monday, Tuesday, every day,
afflicts me, through her means, with bale and ban.
Now are my days but as a painful span;
   nor once "Take heed of dying" did she say.
   I thank you for my life thus cast away,
you who have wearied out a living man.
Yet, oh! my Lord, If I were blessed no more
   than thus much—clothed with your humility,
     to find her for a single hour alone—
such perfectness of joy would triumph over
   this grief wherein I waste, that I should be
     as a new image of Love to look upon.

Terino da Castel
Sonnet: To Onesto da Boncima, in answer to the foregoing

If, as you say, your love torments you,
    that you thereby were in the fear of death,
Messer Onesto, could you bear to be
    far from Love's self, and breathing other breath?
No, you would pass beyond the greater sea
    (I do not speak of the Alps, an easy path),
for your life's gladdening; if so to see
    that light which for my life no comfort has,
but rather makes my grief the bitterer:
    for I have neither ford nor bridge—no course
to reach my lady, or send word to her.
And there is not a greater pain, I think,
    than to see waters at the limpid source,
and to be much athirst, and not to drink

Dante da Maiano
Sonnet: To his lady Nina, of Sicily

So greatly your great pleasaunce pleasured me,
    gentle my lady, from the first of all,
    that counting every other blessing small
I gave myself up wholly to know you:
and since I was made yours, your courtesy
    and worth, more than of earth, celestial,
    I learned, and from its freedom did enthrall
my heart, the servant of your grace to be.
Whereof I pray you, joyful countenance,
    humbly, that it incense or irk you not,
if I, being yours, do wait upon your glance.
More to solicit, I am all afraid:
    yet, lady, twofold is the gift, we wot,
given to the needy unsolicited.

Dante da Maiano

Sonnet: *He thanks his lady for the joy he has had from her*

Wonderful countenance and royal neck,
   I have not found your beauty's parallel!
   nor at her birth might any yet prevail
the likeness of these features to partake.
Wisdom is theirs, and mildness: for whose sake
   All grace seems stolen, such perfect grace to swell;
   fashioned of God beyond delight to dwell
exalted. And herein my pride I take
who of this garden have possession,
   so that all worth subsists for my behoof
     and bears itself according to my will.
     Lady, in you such pleasaunce has its fill
that whoso is content to rest thereon
   knows not grief, and holds all pain aloof.

Guido Guinicelli

Sonnet: *Concerning Lucy*

When Lucy draws her mantle round her face,
   so sweeter than all else she is to see,
   that hence unto the hills there lives not he
whose whole soul would not love her for her grace.
Then seems she like a daughter of some race
   that holds high rule in France or Germany:
   and a snake's head stricken off suddenly
throbs never as then throbs my heart to embrace
her body in these arms, even were she loathe—
   to kiss her lips, to kiss her cheeks, to kiss
     the lids of her two eyes which are two flames.
     Yet what my heart so longs for, my heart blames:
   for surely sorrow might be bred from this
where some man's patient love abides its growth.

DANTE ALIGHIERI

Sonnet: Of Beatrice de' Portinari, on All Saints' Day

Last All Saints' holy-day, even now gone by,
   I met a gathering of damozels:
   she that came first, as one does who excels,
had Love with her, bearing her company:
a flame burned forward through her steadfast eye,
   as when in living fire a spirit dwells:
   so, gazing with the boldness which prevails
over doubt, I knew an angel visibly.
As she passed on, she bowed her mild approof
   and salutation to all men of worth,
lifting the soul to solemn thoughts aloof.
   In Heaven itself that lady had her birth,
I think, and is with us for our behoof:
blessed are they who meet her on the earth.

DINO FRESCOBALDI

Sonnet: Of what his lady is

This is the damsel by whom love is brought
   to enter at his eyes that looks on her;
   this is the righteous maid, the comforter,
whom every virtue honors unbesought.
Love, journeying with her, unto smiles is wrought,
   showing the glory which surrounds her there;
   who, when a lowly heart prefers its prayer,
can make that its transgression come to nought.
And, when she gives greeting, by Love's rule,
   with sweet reserve she somewhat lifts her eyes,
   bestowing that desire which speaks to us.
   Alone on what is noble looks she thus,
   its opposite rejecting in like wise,
this pitiful young maiden beautiful.

DINO FRESCOBALDI

Sonnet: *Of the star of his love*

That star the highest seen in heaven's expanse
    not yet forsakes me with its lovely light:
    it gave me her who from her heaven's pure height
gives all grace my intellect demands.
Thence a new arrow of strength is in my hands
    which bears good will whereso it may alight;
    so barbed, that no man's body or soul its flight
has wounded yet, nor shall wound any man's.
Glad am I therefore that her grace should fall
    not otherwise than thus; whose rich increase
      is such a power as evil cannot dim.
My sins within an instant perished all
    when I inhaled the light of so much peace.
      And this Love knows; for I have told it him.

CINO DA PISTOIA

Madrigal: *To his lady Selvaggia Vergiolesi;*
likening his love to a search for gold

I am all bent to glean the golden ore
    little by little from the riverbed;
      hoping the day to see
when Croesus shall be conquered in my store.
    Therefore, still sifting where the sands are spread,
      I labor patiently:
till, thus intent on this thing and no more—
    if to a vein of silver I were led,
      it scarce could gladden me.
And, seeing that no joy's so warm in the core
    as this whereby the heart is comforted
      and the desire set free—

Cino da Pistoia

Sonnet: Death is not without but within him

This fairest lady, who, as well I wot,
    found entrance by her beauty to my soul,
pierced through my eyes my heart, which erst was whole,
sorely, yet makes as though she knew it not;
nay, turns upon me now, to anger wrought;
    dealing me harshness for my pain's best dole,
    and is so changed by her own wrath's control,
that I go thence, in my distracted thought
content to die; and, mourning, cry abroad
    on Death, as upon one afar from me;
        but Death makes answer from within my heart.
    Then, hearing her so hard at hand to be,
I do commend my spirit unto God;
        saying to her too, "Ease and peace you are."

Cecco's Father

CECCO ANGIOLIERI

Sonnet: *To Messer Angiolieri, his father*

If I'd a sack of florins, and all new,
    (packed tight together, freshly coined and fine)
    and Arcidosso and Montegiovi mine,
and quite a glut of eagle-pieces too—
it were but as three farthings to my view
    without Becchina. Why then all these plots
    to whip me, daddy? Nay, but tell me—what's
my sin, or all the sins of Turks, to you?
For I protest (or may I be struck dead!)
    my love's so firmly planted in its place,
        whipping nor hanging now could change the grain.
And if you want my reason on this head,
    it is that whoso looks her in the face,
        though he were old, gets back his youth again.

CECCO ANGIOLIERI
Sonnet: *Concerning his father*

The dreadful and the desperate hate I bear
    my father (to my praise, not to my shame)
    will make him live more than Methusalem;
of this I've long ago been made aware.
Now tell me, Nature, if my hate's not fair,
    a glass of some thin wine not worth a name
    one day I begged (he has whole butts o' the same)
and he had almost killed me, I declare.
"Good Lord, if I had asked for vernage-wine!"
    said I; for if he'd spit into my face
        I wished to see for reasons of my own.
Now say that I mayn't hate this plague of mine!
    Why, if you knew what I know of his ways,
        you'd tell me that I ought to knock him down.

CECCO ANGIOLIERI
Sonnet: *Of his four tormentors*

I'm caught, like any thrush the nets surprise,
    by Daddy and Becchina, Mammy and Love.
As to the first-named, let thus much suffice—
    each day he damns me, and each hour thereof;
Becchina wants so much of all that's nice,
    not Mahomet himself could yield enough:
and Love still sets me doting in a trice
    on trulls who'd seem the Ghetto's proper stuff.
My mother don't do much because she can't,
    but I may count it just as good as done,
knowing the way and not the will's her want.
Today I tried a kiss with her—just one—
to see if I could make her sulks avaunt:
she said, "The devil rip you up, my son!"

CECCO ANGIOLIERI
Sonnet: On the death of his father

Let not the inhabitants of Hell despair,
    for one's got out who seemed to be locked in;
    and Cecco's the poor devil that I mean,
who thought forever and ever to be there.
But the leaf's turned at last, and I declare
    that now my state of glory does begin:
    for Messer Angiolieri's slipped his skin,
who plagued me, summer and winter, many a year.
Make haste to Cecco, Sonnet, with a will,
    to him who no more at the Abbey dwells;
        tell him that Brother Henry's half dried up.
He'll never more be down-at-mouth, but fill
    his beak at his own beck, till his life swells
        to more than Enoch's or Elijah's scope.

CECCO ANGIOLIERI
Sonnet: He would slay all who hate their fathers

Who utters of his father aught but praise,
    'twere well to cut his tongue out of his mouth;
    because the Deadly Sins are seven, yet does
no one provoke such ire as this must raise.
Were I a priest, or monk in anyways,
    unto the Pope my first respects were paid,
    saying, "Holy Father, let a just crusade
scourge each man who his sire's good name gainsays."
And if by chance a handful of such rogues
    at any time should come into our clutch,
        I'd have them cooked and eaten then and there,
if not by men, at least by wolves and dogs.
    The Lord forgive me! for I fear me much
        some words of mine were rather foul than fair.

Affairs of the Heart

DANTE ALIGHIERI
Sonnet: Of beauty and duty

Two ladies to the summit of my mind
    have clomb, to hold an argument of love.
    The one has wisdom with her from above,
for every noblest virtue well designed:
the other, beauty's tempting power refined
    and the high charm of perfect grace approve:
    and I, as my sweet Master's will does move,
at feet of both their favors am reclined.
Beauty and Duty in my soul keep strife,
    at question if the heart such course can take
    and 'twixt two ladies hold its love complete.
    The fount of gentle speech yields answer meet,
    that Beauty may be loved for gladness' sake,
and Duty in the lofty ends of life.

Guido Guinicelli

Canzone: Of the gentle heart

Within the gentle heart Love shelters him
    as birds within the green shade of the grove.
Before the gentle heart, in nature's scheme,
    Love was not, nor the gentle heart ere Love.
    For with the sun, at once,
so sprang the light immediately; nor was
    its birth before the sun's.
And Love has his effect in gentleness
    of very self; even as
within the middle fire the heat's excess.

The fire of Love comes to the gentle heart
    like as its virtue to a precious stone;
to which no star its influence can impart
    till it is made a pure thing by the sun:
    for when the sun has smit
from out its essence that which there was vile,
    the star endows it.
And so the heart created by God's breath
    pure, true, and clean from guile,
a woman, like a star, enamors.

In gentle heart Love for like reason is
    for which the lamp's high flame is fanned and bowed:
clear, piercing bright, it shines for its own bless;
    nor would it burn there else, it is so proud.
    For evil natures meet
with Love as it were water met with fire,
    as cold abhorring heat.
Through gentle heart Love does a track divine—
    like knowing like; the same
as diamond runs through iron in the mine.

The sun strikes full upon the mud all day:
    it remains vile, nor the sun's worth is less.
"By race I am gentle," the proud man does say:
    he is the mud, the sun is gentleness.
    Let no one predicate
that aught the name of gentleness should have,
    even in a king's estate,

Except the heart there be a gentle man's.
           The star-beam lights the wave—
Heaven holds the star and the star's radiance.

God, in the understanding of high Heaven,
    burns more than in our sight the living sun:
there to behold His Face unveiled is given;
    and Heaven, whose will is homage paid to One,
        fulfills the things which live
in God, from the beginning excellent.
        So should my lady give
that truth which in her eyes is glorified,
        on which her heart is bent,
to me whose service waits at her side.

My lady, God shall ask, "What dare you?"
    (when my soul stands with all her acts reviewed)
"You passed Heaven, into My sight, as now,
    to make Me of vain love similitude.
        To Me does praise belong,
and to the Queen of all the realm of grace
        who slays fraud and wrong."
Then may I plead: "As though from You he came,
        Love wore an angel's face:
Lord, if I loved her, count it not my shame."

Cecco Angiolieri

Sonnet: *He will not be too deeply in love*

I am enamored, and yet not so much
    but that I'd do without it easily;
    and my own mind thinks all the more of me
that Love has not quite penned me in his hutch.
Enough if for his sake I dance and touch
    the lute, and serve his servants cheerfully:
    an overdose is worse than none would be:
Love is no lord of mine, I'm proud to vouch.
So let no woman who is born conceive
    that I'll be her liege slave, as I see some,
    be she as fair and dainty as she will.
Too much of love makes idiots, I believe:
    I like not any fashion that turns glum
        the heart, and makes the visage sick and ill.

Guido Cavalcanti

Canzone: *He laments the presumption and incontinence of his youth*

The devastating flame of that fierce plague,
    the foe of virtue, fed with others' peace
        more than itself foresees,
    being still shut in to gnaw its own desire;
its strength not weakened, nor its hues more vague,
    for all the benison that virtue sheds,
        but which forever spreads
    to be a living curse that shall not tire:
    or yet again, that other idle fire
which flickers with all change as winds may please:
        one whichsoever of these
at length has hidden the true path from me
    which twice man may not see.

Cino da Pistoia

Sonnet: To Love, in great bitterness

O Love, O you that, for my fealty,
    only in torment does your power employ,
    give me, for God's sake, something of your joy,
that I may learn what good there is in you.
Yea, for, if you are glad with grieving me,
    surely my very life you shall destroy
    when you renew my pain, because the joy
must then be wept for with the misery.
He that had never sense of good, nor sight,
    esteems his ill estate but natural,
        which so is lightlier borne: his case is mine.
    But, if you would uplift me for a sign,
    bidding me drain the curse and know it all,
I must a little taste its opposite.

Dante Alighieri

Sonnet to Cino da Pistoia: He rebukes Cino for fickleness

I thought to be forever separate,
    fair Master Cino, from these rhymes of yours;
    since further from the coast, another course,
my vessel now must journey with her freight.
Yet still, because I hear men name your state
    as his whom every lure does straight beguile,
    I pray you lend a very little while
unto my voice your ear grown obdurate.
The man after this measure amorous,
    who still at his own will is bound and loosed,
        how slightly Love him wounds is lightly known.
If on this wise your heart in homage bows,
    I pray you for God's sake it be disused,
        So that the deed and the sweet words be one.

Cino da Pistoia

Sonnet: *He answers Dante, confessing his unsteadfast heart*

Dante, since I from my own native place
    in heavy exile have turned wanderer,
    far distant from the purest joy which ever
had issued from the Fount of joy and grace,
I have gone weeping through the world's dull space,
    and me proud Death, as one too mean, does spare;
    yet meeting Love, Death's neighbor, I declare
that still his arrows hold my heart in chase.
Nor from his pitiless aim can I get free,
    nor from the hope which comforts my weak will,
        though no true aid exists which I could share.
One pleasure ever binds and looses me;
    that so, by one same Beauty lured, I still
        delight in many women here and there.

Guido Guinicelli

Sonnet: *Of moderation and tolerance*

He that has grown to wisdom hurries not,
    but thinks and weighs what Reason bids him do
and after thinking he retains his thought
    until as he conceived the fact ensue.
Let no one to overweening pride be wrought,
    but count his state as Fortune's gift and due.
He is a fool who deems that none has sought
    the truth, save he alone, or knows it true.
Many strange birds are on the air abroad,
    nor all are of one flight or of one force,
    but each after his kind dissimilar;
to each was portioned of the breath of God,
    who gave them diverse instincts from one source.
        Then judge not you your fellows what they are.

CECCO ANGIOLIERI

Sonnet: Of love in men and devils

The man who feels not, more or less, somewhat
   of love in all the years his life goes round
   should be denied a grave in holy ground
except with usurers who will bate no groat;
nor he himself should count himself a jot
    less wretched than the meanest beggar found.
   Also the man who in Love's robe is gowned
may say that Fortune smiles upon his lot.
Seeing how love has such nobility
    that if it entered in the lord of Hell
      'twould rule him more than his fire's ancient sting;
he should be glorified to eternity,
    and all his life be always glad and well
      as is a wanton woman in the spring.

GUIDO GUINICELLI

Canzone: He perceives his rashness in love, but has no choice

I hold him, verily, of mean emprise,
    whose rashness tempts a strength too great to bear;
as I have done, alas! who turned my eyes
    upon those perilous eyes of the most fair.
        Unto her eyes I bowed;
no need her other beauties in that hour
        should aid them, cold and proud:
as when the vassals of a mighty lord,
    what time he needs his power,
are all girt round him to make strong his sword.

With such exceeding force the stroke was dealt
    that by my eyes its path might not be stayed;
but deep into the heart it pierced, which felt
    the pang of the sharp wound, and waxed afraid;
        then rested in strange wise,
as when some creature utterly outworn
        sinks into bed and lies.
And she the while does in no manner care,
    but goes her way in scorn,
beholding herself always proud and fair.

And she may be as proud as she shall please,
    for she is still the fairest woman found:
a sun she seems among the rest; and these
    have all their beauties in her splendour drowned.
        In her is every grace—
simplicity of wisdom, noble speech,
        accomplished loveliness;
all earthly beauty is her diadem,
    this truth my song would teach—
my lady is of ladies chosen gem.

Love to my lady's service yields me—
    will I, or will I not, the thing is so—
nor other reason can I say or see,
    except that where it lists the wind does blow.
        He rules and gives no sign;

> nor once from her did show of love upbuoy
>> this passion which is mine.
> It is because her virtue's strength and stir
>> so fill her full of joy
> that I am glad to die for love of her.

Dreams and Images

CINO DA PISTOIA

Sonnet: A trance of Love

Vanquished and weary was my soul in me,
    and my heart gasped after its much lament,
    when sleep at length the painful languor sent.
And, as I slept (and wept incessantly)—
through the keen fixedness of memory
    which I had cherished ere my tears were spent,
    I passed to a new trance of wonderment;
wherein a visible spirit I could see,
which caught me up, and bore me to a place
    where my most gentle lady was alone;
        and still before us a fire seemed to move,
    out of the which methought there came a moan
uttering, "Grace, a little season, grace!
    I am of one that has the wings of Love."

Dante da Maiano

Sonnet: He craves interpreting of a dream of his

You that are wise, let wisdom minister
    unto my dream, that it be understood.
To wit: A lady, of her body fair,
    and whom my heart approves in womanhood,
    bestowed on me a wreath of flowers, fair-hued
and green in leaf, with gentle loving air;
    and the which, meseemed I was stark nude
save for a smock of hers that I did wear.
Whereat, good friend, my courage gat such growth
    that to my arms I took her tenderly:
with no rebuke the beauty laughed unloth,
    and as she laughed I kissed continually.
I say no more, for that I pledged my oath,
    and that my mother, who is dead, was by.

Guido Orlandi

Sonnet: He interprets the dream
related in the foregoing sonnet

On the last words of what you write to me
    I give you my opinion at the first,
    to see the dead must prove corruption nursed
within you, by your heart's own vanity.
The soul should bend the flesh to its decree:
    then rule it, friend, as fish by line amerced.
    As to the smock, your lady's gift, the worst
of words were not too bad for speech so free.
It is a thing unseemly to declare
    the love of gracious dame or damozel,
        and therewith for excuse to say, I dreamed.
        Tell us no more of this, but think who seemed
    to call you; mother came to whip you well.
Love close, and of Love's joy you'll have your share.

Cecco Angiolieri

Sonnet: Of all he would do

If I were fire, I'd burn the world away;
    if I were wind, I'd turn my storms thereon;
    if I were water, I'd soon let it drown;
if I were God, I'd sink it from the day;
if I were Pope, I'd never feel quite gay
    until there was no peace beneath the sun;
    if I were Emperor, what would I have done?—
I'd lop men's heads all round in my own way.
If I were Death, I'd look my father up;
    if I were Life, I'd run away from him;
        and treat my mother to like calls and runs.
If I were Cecco (and that's all my hope),
    I'd pick the nicest girls to suit my whim,
        and other folk should get the ugly ones.

Guido Cavalcanti

Sonnet to Guido Orlandi: Of a consecrated image resembling his lady

Guido, an image of my lady dwells,
    at San Michele in Orto, consecrate
    and duly worshipped. Fair in holy state
she listens to the tale each sinner tells:
and among them that come to her, who ails
    the most, on him the most does blessing wait.
    She bids the fiend men's bodies abdicate;
over the curse of blindness she prevails,
and heals sick languors in the public squares.
    A multitude adores her reverently:
        before her face two burning tapers are;
        her voice is uttered upon paths afar.
    Yet through the Lesser Brethren's jealousy
she is named idol; not being one of theirs.

Guido Orlandi

Madrigal to Guido Cavalcanti:
In answer to the foregoing sonnet

If you had offered, friend, to blessed Mary
      a pious voluntary,
    as thus: "Fair rose, in holy garden set,"
you then had found a true similitude;
      because all truth and good
    are hers, who was the mansion and the gate
wherein abode our high salvation,
      conceived in her, a son,
    even by the angel's greeting whom she met.
Be you assured that if one cry to her,
      confessing, "I did err,"
    for death she gives him life; for she is great.
Ah! how may you be counselled to implead
      with God your own misdeed,
    and not another's? Ponder what you are;
      and humbly lay to heart
that publican who wept his proper need.
The Lesser Brethren cherish the divine
      scripture and church-doctrine;
being appointed keepers of the faith
      whose preaching succours:
for what they preach is our best medicine.

Vita Nuova

Sonnet to Brunetto Latini

sent with
the *Vita Nuova*

Master Brunetto, this my little maid
is come to spend her Easter-tide with you:
not that she reckons feasting as her due—
whose need is hardly to be fed, but read.

Not in a hurry can her sense be weighed,
nor mid the jests of any noisy crew:
Ah! and she wants a little coaxing too
before she'll get into another's head.

But if you do not find her meaning clear,
you've many Brother Alberts hard at hand,
    whose wisdom will respond to any call.

Consult with them and do not laugh at her;
and if she still is hard to understand,
    apply to Master Janus last of all.

The New Life

Dante's
poems
and
exposition
of Love

IN THAT PART OF THE BOOK OF MY MEMORY before which is little that can be read, there is a rubric, saying, *Incipit Vita Nova* [Here begins the new life, or my young life]. Under such rubric I find written many things; and among them the words which I purpose to copy into this little book; if not all of them, at the least their substance.

    Nine times already since my birth had the heaven of light returned to the self-same point almost, as concerns its own revolution, when first the glorious Lady of my mind was made manifest to my eyes; even she who was called Beatrice [she who confers blessing] by many who knew not wherefore. She had already been in this life for so long as that, within her time, the starry heaven had moved toward the Eastern quarter one of the twelve parts of a degree; so that she appeared to me at the beginning of her ninth year almost, and I saw her almost at the end of my ninth year. Her dress, on that day, was of a most noble color, a subdued and goodly crimson, girdled and adorned in such sort as best suited with her very tender age. At that moment, I say most truly that the spirit of life, which has its dwelling in the secretest chamber of the heart, began to tremble so violently that the least pulses of my body shook therewith; and in trembling it said these words: *Ecce deus fortior me, qui veniens dominabitur mihi* [Here is a deity stronger than I; who, coming, shall rule over me]. At that moment the animate spirit, which dwells in the lofty chamber where all the senses carry their perceptions, was filled with wonder, and speaking more especially unto the spirits of the eyes, said these words: *Apparuit iam beatitudo vestra* [Your beatitude has now been made manifest unto you]. At that moment the natural spirit, which dwells there where our nourishment is administered, began to weep, and in weeping said these words: *Heu miser! quia frequenter impeditus ero deinceps!* [Woe is me! for that often I shall be disturbed from this time forth!]

I say that, from that time forward, Love quite governed my soul; which was immediately espoused to him, and with so safe and undisputed a lordship (by virtue of strong imagination) that I had nothing left for it but to do all his bidding continually. He oftentimes commanded me to seek if I might see this youngest of the Angels: wherefore I in my boyhood often went in search of her, and found her so noble and praiseworthy that certainly of her might have been said those words of the poet Homer, "She seemed not to be the daughter of a mortal man, but of God" [Οὐδὲ ἐῴκει Ἀνδπός γε θνητοῦ παῖς ἔμμεναι, ἀλλὰ θεοῖο. (*Iliad*, xxiv. 258)]. And albeit her image, that was with me always, was an exultation of Love to subdue me, it was yet of so perfect a quality that it never allowed me to be overruled by Love without the faithful counsel of reason, whensoever such counsel was useful to be heard. But seeing that were I to dwell overmuch on the passions and doings of such early youth, my words might be counted something fabulous, I will therefore put them aside; and passing many things that may be conceived by the pattern of these, I will come to such as are writ in my memory with a better distinctness.

After the lapse of so many days that nine years exactly

were completed since the above-written appearance of this most gracious being, on the last of those days it happened that the same wonderful lady appeared to me dressed all in pure white, between two gentle ladies elder than she. And passing through a street, she turned her eyes where I stood sorely abashed: and by her unspeakable courtesy, which is now guerdoned in the Great Cycle, she saluted me with so virtuous a bearing that I seemed then and there to behold the very limits of blessedness. The hour of her most sweet salutation was exactly the ninth of that day; and because it was the first time that any words from her reached my ears, I came into such sweetness that I parted thence as one intoxicated. And betaking me to the loneliness of my own room, I fell to thinking of this most courteous lady, thinking of whom I was overtaken by a pleasant slumber, wherein a marvellous vision was presented for me: for there appeared to be in my room a mist of the color of fire, within which I discerned the figure of a lord of terrible aspect to such as should gaze upon him, but who seemed therewithal to rejoice inwardly that it was a marvel to see. Speaking he said many things, among the which I could understand but few; and of these, this: *Ego dominus tuus* [I am your master]. In his arms it seemed to me that a person was sleeping, covered only with a blood-colored cloth; upon whom looking very attentively, I knew that it was the lady of the salutation who had deigned the day before to salute me. And he who held her held also in his hand a thing that was burning in flames; and he said to me, *Vide cor tuum* [Behold your heart]. But when he had remained with me a little while, I thought that he set himself to awaken her that slept; after the which he made her to eat that thing which flamed in his hand; and she ate as one fearing. Then, having waited again a space, all his joy was turned into most bitter weeping; and as he wept he gathered the lady into his arms, and it seemed to me that he went with her up towards heaven: whereby such a great anguish came upon me that my light slumber could not endure through it, but was suddenly broken.

And immediately having considered, I knew that the hour wherein this vision had been made manifest to me was the fourth hour (which is to say, the first of the nine last hours) of the night.

Then, musing on what I had seen, I proposed to relate the same to many poets who were famous in that day: and for that I had myself in some sort the art of discoursing with rhyme, I resolved on making a sonnet, in which, having saluted all such as are subject unto Love, and entreated them to expound my vision, I should write unto them those things which I had seen in my sleep. And the sonnet I made was this:

> This sonnet is divided into two parts. In the first part I give greeting, and ask an answer.

To every heart which the sweet pain does move,
and unto which these words may now be brought
for true interpretation and kind thought,
be greeting in our Lord's name, which is Love.
Of those long hours wherein the stars, above,
wake and keep watch, the third was almost
    nought,
when Love was shown me with such terrors
    fraught
as may not carelessly be spoken of.
He seemed like one who is full of joy, and had
my heart within his hand, and on his arm
my lady, with a mantle round her, slept;
whom (having wakened her) anon he made
to eat that heart; she ate, as fearing harm.
Then he went out; and as he went, he wept.

The second part commences here:

In the second I signify what thing has to be answered to.

To this sonnet I received many answers, conveying many different opinions; of which one was sent by him whom I now call the first among my friends [Guido Cavalcanti], and it began thus, "Unto my thinking you beheld all worth." And indeed, it was when he learned that I was he who had sent those rhymes to him, that our friendship commenced. But the true meaning of that vision was not then perceived by anyone, though it be now evident to the least skillful.

From that night forth, the natural functions of my body began to be vexed and impeded, for I was given up wholly to thinking of this most gracious creature: whereby in short space I became so weak and so reduced that it was irksome to many of my friends to look upon me; while others, being moved by spite, went about to discover what it was my wish should be concealed. Wherefore I (perceiving the drift of their unkindly questions), by Love's will, who directed me according to the counsels of reason, told them how it was Love himself who had thus dealt with me: and I said so, because the thing was so plainly to be discerned in my countenance that there was no longer any means of concealing it. But when they went on to ask, "And by whose help hath Love done this?" I looked in their faces smiling, and spake no word in return.

Now it fell on a day, that this most gracious creature was sitting where words were to be heard of the Queen of Glory; and I was in a place where mine eyes could behold their beatitude: and between her and me, in a direct line, there sat another lady of a pleasant favor; who looked round at me many times, marvelling at my continued gaze which seemed to have her for its object. And many perceived that she thus looked; so that departing thence, I heard it whispered after me "Look you to what a pass such a lady has brought him"; and in saying this they named her who had been midway between the most gentle Beatrice and mine eyes. Therefore I was reassured, and knew that for that day my secret had not become manifest. Then immediately it came into my mind that I might make use of this lady as a screen to the truth: and so well did I play my part that the most of those who had hitherto watched and wondered at me, now imagined they had found me out. By her means I kept my secret concealed till some years were gone over; and for my better security, I even made diverse rhymes in her honor; whereof I shall here write only as much as concerned the most gentle Beatrice, which is but a very little. Moreover, about the same time while this lady was a screen for so much love on my part, I took the resolution to set down the name of this most gracious creature accompanied with the many other women's names, and especially with hers whom I spoke of. And to this end I put together the names of sixty of the most beautiful ladies in that city where God had placed my own lady; and these names I introduced in an epistle in the form of a sirvent, which it is not my intention to transcribe here. Neither should I have said anything of this matter, did I not wish to take note of a certain strange thing, to wit: that having written the list, I found my lady's name would not stand otherwise than ninth in order among the names of these ladies.

 Now it so chanced with her by whose means I had thus long time concealed my desire, that it behoved her to leave the city I speak of, and to journey afar: wherefore I, being sorely perplexed at the loss of so excellent a defense, had more trouble than even I could before have supposed. And thinking that if I spoke not somewhat mournfully of her departure, my former counterfeiting would be the more quickly perceived, I determined that I would make a grievous sonnet thereof; the which I will write here, because it has certain words in it whereof my lady was the immediate cause, as will be plain to him that understands. And the sonnet was this:—

This poem has two principal parts; for, in the first I mean to call the Faithful of Love in those words of Jeremias the Prophet, *O vos omnes qui transitis per viam, attendite et videte si este dolor sicut dolor meus*, and to pray them to stay and hear me.

> All you that pass along Love's trodden way,
> Pause you awhile and say
> If there be any grief like unto mine:
> I pray you that you hearken a short space
> Patiently, if my case
> Be not a piteous marvel and a sign.
>
> Love (never, certainly, for my worthless part,
> But of his own great heart),
> Vouchsafed to me a life so calm and sweet
> That oft I heard folk question as I went
> What such great gladness meant:—
> They spoke of it behind me in the street.
>
> But now that fearless bearing is all gone
> Which with Love's hoarded wealth was
>   given me;
> Till I am grown to be
> So poor that I have dread to think thereon.
>
> And thus it is that I, being like as one
> Who is ashamed and hides his poverty.
> Without seem full of glee,
> And let my heart within travail and moan.

The second part begins here:

➡ *In the second I tell where Love had placed me, with a meaning other than that which the last part*

A certain while after the departure of that lady, it pleased the Master of the Angels to call into His glory a damsel, young and of a gentle presence, who had been very lovely in the city I speak of: and I saw her body lying without its soul among many ladies who held a pitiful weeping. Whereupon, remembering that I had seen her in the company of excellent Beatrice, I could not hinder myself from a few tears; and weeping, I conceived to say somewhat of her death, in guerdon of having seen her somewhile with my lady; which thing I spoke of in the latter end of the verses that I write in this matter, as he will discern who understands. And I wrote two sonnets, which are these:

> This first sonnet is divided into three parts. In the first, I call and beseech the Faithful of Love to weep; and I say that their Lord weeps, and that they, hearing the reason why he weeps, shall be more minded to listen to me.

I

Weep, Lovers, since Love's very self does weep,
and since the cause for weeping is so great;
when now so many dames, of such estate
in worth, show with their eyes a grief so deep.

For Death the churl has laid his leaden sleep
upon a damsel who was fair of late,
defacing all our earth should celebrate—
yea all save virtue, which the soul does keep.

Now hearken how much Love did honor her.
I myself saw him in his proper form
    bending above the motionless sweet dead,
and often gazing into Heaven; for there
the soul now sits which when her life was warm
    dwelt with the joyful beauty that is fled.

← In the second, I relate this reason.

← In the third, I speak of honor done by Love to this Lady.

This poem is divided into four parts. In the first I address Death by certain proper names of hers.

In the second, speaking to her, I tell the reason why I am moved to denounce her.

In the third, I rail against her.

In the fourth, ➡ I turn to speak to a person undefined, although defined in my own

II

Death, always cruel, Pity's foe in chief,
mother who brought forth grief,
    merciless judgment and without appeal!
    Since you alone have made my heart to feel
    this sadness and unweal,
my tongue upbraids you without relief.
And now (for I must rid your name of ruth)
behoves me speak the truth
    touching your cruelty and wickedness:
    not that they be not known: but nevertheless
    I would give hate more stress
with them that feed on love in very sooth.
Out of this world you have driven courtesy,
    and virtue, dearly prized in womanhood;
    and out of youth's gay mood
the lovely lightness is quite gone through you.

Whom now I mourn, no one shall learn from me
    save by the measure of these praises given.
    Whoso deserves not Heaven
may never hope to have her company.

Some days after the death of this lady, I had occasion to leave the city I speak of, and to go where she abode who had formerly been my protection; albeit the end of my journey reached not altogether so far. And notwithstanding that I was visibly in the company of many, the journey was so irksome that I had scarcely sighing enough to ease my heart's heaviness; seeing that as I went, I left my beatitude behind me. Wherefore it came to pass that he who ruled me by virtue of my most gentle lady was made visible to my mind, in the light habit of a traveller, coarsely fashioned. He appeared to me troubled, and looked always on the ground; saving only that sometimes his eyes were turned towards a river which was clear and rapid, and which flowed along the path I was taking. And then I thought that Love called me and said to me these words: "I come from that lady who was so long your surety; for the matter of whose return, I know that it may not be. Wherefore I have taken that heart which I made you leave with her, and do bear it unto another lady, who, as she was, shall be your surety"; (and when he named her I knew her well). "And of these words I have spoken if you should speak any again, let it be in such sort as that none shall perceive thereby that your love was feigned for her, which you must now feign for another." And when he had spoken thus, all my imagining was gone suddenly, for it seemed to me that Love became a part of myself: so that, changed as it were in mine aspect, I rode on full of thought the whole of that day, and with heavy sighing. And the day being over, I wrote this sonnet:

This sonnet has three parts. In the first part, I tell how I met love, and of his aspect.

In the second, ➡ I tell what he said to me, although not in full, through the fear I had of discovering my secret.

In the third, ➡ I say how he disappeared.

> A day agone, as I rode sullenly
> Upon a certain path that liked me not,
> I met Love midway while the air was hot,
> Clothed lightly as a wayfarer might be.
> And for the cheer he showed, he seemed to me
> As one who has lost lordship he had got;
> Advancing towards me full of sorrowful
>   thought,
> Bowing his forehead so that none should see
> Then as I went, he called me by my name,
>   Saying: "I journey since the morn was dim
>   Thence where I made your heart to be:
>   which now
> I needs must bear unto another dame."
>   Wherewith so much passed into me of him
>   That he was gone, and I discerned not how.

On my return, I set myself to seek out that lady whom my master had named to me while I journeyed sighing. And because I would be brief, I will now narrate that in a short while I made her my surety, in such sort that the matter was spoken of by many in terms scarcely courteous; through the which I had oftenwhiles many troublesome hours. And by this it happened (to wit: by this false and evil rumor which seemed to misfame me of vice) that she who was the destroyer of all evil and the queen of all good, coming where I was, denied me her most sweet salutation, in the which alone was my blessedness.

And here it is fitting for me to depart a little from this present matter, that it may be rightly understood of what surpassing virtue her salutation was to me. To the which end I say that when she appeared in any place, it seemed to me, by the hope of her excellent salutation, that there was no man my enemy any longer; and such warmth of charity came upon me that most certainly in that moment I would have pardoned whosoever had done me an injury; and if one should then have questioned me concerning any matter, I could only have said unto him "Love," with a countenance clothed in humbleness. And what time she made ready to salute me, the spirit of Love, destroying all other perceptions, thrust forth the feeble spirits of my eyes, saying "Do homage unto your mistress," and putting itself in their place to obey: so that he who would, might then have beheld Love, beholding the lids of my eyes shake. And when this most gentle lady gave her salutation, Love, so far from being a medium beclouding mine intolerable beatitude, then bred in me such an overpowering sweetness that my body, being all subjected thereto,, remained many times helpless and passive. Whereby it is made manifest that in her salutation alone was there any beatitude for me, which then very often went beyond my endurance.

And now, resuming my discourse, I will go on to relate that when, for the first time, this beatitude was denied me, I became possessed with such grief that, parting myself from others, I went into a lonely place to bathe the ground with most bitter tears: and when, by this heat of weeping, I was somewhat relieved, I betook myself to my chamber, where I could lament unheard. And there, having prayed to the Lady of all Mercies, and having said also, "O Love, aid you your servant," I went suddenly asleep, like a beaten sobbing child. And in my sleep, towards the middle of it, I seemed to see in the room, seated at my side, a youth in very white raiment, who kept his eyes fixed on me in deep thought. And when he had gazed some time, I thought that he sighed and called me to me in these words: *Fili mi, tempus est ut praetermittantur simulata nostra* [My son, it is time for us to lay aside our counterfeiting]. And thereupon I seemed to know him; for the voice was the same wherewith he had spoken at other times in my sleep. Then looking at him, I perceived that he was weeping piteously, and that he seemed to be waiting for me to speak. Wherefore, taking heart, I began thus: "Why weep you Master of all honor?" And he made answer to me: *Ego tanquam centrum circuli, cui similis modo se habent circumferentiae partes: tu autem non sic* [I am as the center of a circle, to which all parts of the circumference bear an equal relation: but with you it is not thus]. And thinking upon his words, they seemed to me obscure; so that again compelling myself unto speech, I asked of him: "What thing is this, Master, that you have spoken thus darkly?" To the which he made answer in the vulgar tongue: "Demand no more than may be useful to you." Whereupon I began to discourse with him concerning her salutation which she had denied me; and when I had questioned him of the cause, he said these words: "Our Beatrice has heard from certain persons, that the lady whom I named to you while you journeyed full of sighs is sorely disquieted by your solicitations: and therefore this most gracious creature, who is the enemy of all disquiet, being fearful of such disquiet, refused to salute you. For the which reason (albeit, in very sooth, your secret must needs have become known to hear by familiar observation) it is my will that you compose certain things in rhyme, in the which you shall set forth how strong a mastership I have obtained over you, through her; and how you were hers even from your childhood. Also do you call upon him that knows these things to bear witness to them, bidding him to speak with her thereof; the which I, who am he, will do willingly. And thus she shall be made to know your desire; knowing which, she shall know likewise that they were deceived who spoke of you to hear. And so write these things, that they shall seem rather to be spoken by a third person; and not directly by you to her, which is scarce fitting. After the which, send them, not without me, where she may chance to hear them; but have them fitted with a pleasant music, into which I will pass whensoever it needs." With this speech he was away, and my sleep was broken up.

Whereupon, remembering me, I knew that I had beheld this vision during the ninth hour of the day; and I resolved that I would made a ditty, before I left my chamber, according to the words my master had spoken. And this is the ditty that I made:

This ditty is divided into three parts. In the first, I tell it whither to go, and I encourage it, that it may go the more confidently, and I tell it whose company to join if it would go with confidence and without any danger.

In the 2nd, ➡ I say that which it behoves the ditty to set forth.

Song, 'tis my will that you do seek out Love,
and go with him where my dear lady is;
that so my cause, the which your harmonies
do plead, his better speech may clearly prove.

You go, my Song, in such a courteous kind,
that even companionless
    you may rely on yourself anywhere.
And yet, if you would get you a safe mind,
first unto Love address
    your steps; whose aid, mayhap, 'twere ill to spare,
    seeing that she to whom you make your prayer
is, as I think, ill-minded unto me,
and that if Love do not companion you
You'll have perchance small cheer to tell me of.

With a sweet accent, when you come to her,
begin you in these words,
    first having craved a gracious audience:
"He who has sent me as his messenger,
Lady, thus much records,
    if you but suffer him, in his defense.
    Love, who comes with me, by your influence
Can make this man do as it likes him:
Wherefore, if this fault is or does but seem
do you conceive: for his heart cannot move."

Say to her also: "Lady, his poor heart
is so confirmed in faith
    that all its thoughts are but of serving you:
'Twas early yours, and could not swerve apart."

Then, if she wavers,
    bid her ask Love, who knows if these things be.
    And in the end, beg of her modestly
to pardon so much boldness: saying too:—
"If you declare his death to be your due,
the thing shall come to pass, as does behove."

Then pray you of the Master of all ruth,
before you leave her there,
    that he befriend my cause and plead it well.
"In guerdon of my sweet rhymes and my truth"
(entreat him) "stay with her;
    let not the hope of thy poor servant fail;
    and if with her your pleading should prevail,
let her look on him and give peace to him."

Gentle my Song, if good to you it seem,
Do this: so worship shall be yours and love.

← In the third, I give it leave to start when it pleases, recommending its course to the arms of Fortune. Some might contradict me, and say that they understand not whom I address in the second person, seeing that the ditty is merely the very words I am speaking. And therefore I say that this doubt I intend to solve and clear up in this little book itself, at a more difficult passage, and then let him understand who now doubts, or would now contradict as aforesaid.

After this vision I have recorded, and having written those words which Love had dictated to me, I began to be harassed with many and divers thoughts, by each of which I was sorely tempted; and in especial, there were four among them that left me no rest. The first was this: "Certainly the lordship of Love is good; seeing that it diverts the mind from all mean things." The second was this: "Certainly the lordship of Love is evil; seeing that the more homage his servants pay to him, the more grievous and painful are the torments wherewith he torments them." The third was this: "The name of Love is so sweet in the hearing that it would not seem possible for its effects to be other than sweet; seeing that the name must needs be like unto the thing named: as it is written: *Nonina sunt consequentia rerum* [Names are the consequents of things]. And the fourth was this: "The lady whom Love hath chosen out to govern thee is not as other ladies, whose hearts are easily moved."

And by each one of these thoughts I was so sorely assailed that I was like unto him who doubts which path to take, and wishing to go, goes not. And if I bethought myself to seek out some point at the which all these paths might be found to meet, I discerned but one way, and that irked me: to wit, to call upon Pity, and to commend myself unto her. And it was then that, feeling a desire to write somewhat thereof in rhyme, I wrote this sonnet:

This sonnet may be divided into four parts. In the first, I say and propound that all my thoughts are concerning Love.

> All my thoughts always speak to me of love,
> yet have between themselves such difference
> that while one bids me bow with mind and sense,
> a second says, "Go to: look you above";
> the third one, hoping, yields me joy enough;
> and with the last come tears, I scarce know whence:
> all of them craving pity in sore suspense,
> trembling with fears that the heart knows of.
> And thus, being all unsure which path to take,
> wishing to speak I know not what to say,
> and lose myself in amorous wanderings:
> until (my peace with all of them to make),
> unto my enemy I needs must pray,
> my Lady Pity, for the help she brings.

← In the second, I say that they are diverse, and I relate their diversity.

← In the third, I say wherein they all seem to agree.

← In the fourth, I say that, wishing to speak of Love, I know not from which of these thoughts to take my argument; and that if I would take it from all, I shall have to call upon mine enemy, my Lady Pity. "Lady," I say, as in a scornful mode of speech.

After this battling with many thoughts, it chanced on a day that my most gracious lady was with a gathering of ladies in a certain place; to which I was conducted by a friend of mine; he thinking to do me a great pleasure by showing me the beauty of so many women. Then I, hardly knowing whereunto he conducted me, but trusting in him (who yet was leading his friend to the last verge of life), made question: "To what end are we come among these ladies?" and he answered: "To the end that they may be worthily served." And they were assembled around a gentlewoman who was given in marriage on that day; the custom of the city being that these should bear her company when she sat down for the first time at table in the house of her husband. Therefore I, as was my friend's pleasure, resolved to stay with him and do honor to those ladies.

But as soon as I had thus resolved, I began to feel a faintness and a throbbing at my left side, which soon took possession of my whole body. Whereupon I remember that I covertly leaned my back unto a painting that ran around the walls of that house; and being fearful lest my trembling should be discerned of them, I lifted my eyes to look on those ladies, and then first perceived among them the excellent Beatrice. And when I perceived her, all my senses were overpowered by the great lordship that Love obtained, finding himself so near unto that most gracious being, until nothing but the spirits of sight remained to me; and even these remained driven out of their own instruments, because Love entered in that honored place of theirs, that so he might the better behold her. And although I was other than at first, I grieved for the spirits so expelled, which kept up a sore lament, saying: "If he had not in this wise thrust us forth, we also should behold the marvel of this lady." By this, many of her friends, having discerned my confusion, began to wonder; and together with herself, kept whispering of me and mocking me. Whereupon my friend, who knew not what to conceive, took me by the hands, and drawing me forth from among them, required to know what ailed me. Then, having first held me at quiet for a space until my perceptions were coming back to me, I made answer to my friend: "Of a surety I have now set my feet on that point of life, beyond the which he must not pass who would return."

Afterwards, leaving him, I went back to the room where I had wept before; and again weeping and ashamed, said: "If this lady but knew of my condition, I do not think that she would thus mock at me; nay, I am sure that she must needs feel some pity." And in my weeping I bethought me to write certain words, in the which, speaking to her, I should signify the occasion of my disfigurement, telling her also how I knew that she had no knowledge thereof; which, if it were known, I was certain must move others to pity. And then, because I hoped that peradventure it might come into her hearing, I wrote this sonnet:

Even as the others mock, you mock me;
    not dreaming, noble lady, whence it is
    that I am taken with strange semblances,
seeing your face which is so fair to see:
for else, compassion would not suffer you
    to grieve my heart with such harsh scoffs as these.
    Lo! Love, when you are present, sits at ease,
and bears his mastership so mightily
that all my troubled senses he thrusts out,
    sorely tormenting some, and slaying some,
        till none but he is left and has free range
        to gaze on you. This makes my face to change
    into another's; while I stand all dumb,
and hear my senses clamor in their rout.

> This sonnet I divided not into parts, because a division
> is only made to open the meaning of the thing divided:
> and this, as it is sufficiently manifest through the reasons
> given, has no need of division. True it is that, amid the
> words whereby is shown the occasion of this sonnet,
> dubious words are to be found; namely, when I say that
> Love fills all my spirits, but that the visual remain in life
> only outside of their own instruments. And this difficulty
> it is impossible for any to solve who is not in equal guise
> liege unto Love; and, to those who are so, that is manifest
> which would clear up the dubious words. And therefore
> it were not well for me to expound this difficulty,
> inasmuch as my speaking would be either fruitless or else
> superfluous.

A while after this strange disfigurement, I became possessed with a strong conception which left me but very seldom, and then to return quickly. And it was this: "Seeing that you come into such scorn by the companionship of this lady, wherefore seek you to behold her? If she should ask you this thing, what answer could you make unto her? yes, even though you were master of all your faculties, and in no way hindered from answering." Unto which, another very humble thought said in reply: "If I were master of all my faculties, and in no way hindered from answering, I would tell her that no sooner do I image to myself her marvelous beauty than I am possessed with the desire to behold her, which is of so great strength that it kills and destroys in my memory all those things which might oppose it; and it is therefore that the great anguish I have endured thereby is yet not enough to restrain me from seeking to behold her." And then, because of these thoughts, I resolved to write somewhat, wherein, having pleaded mine excuse, I should tell her of what I felt in her presence. Whereupon I wrote this sonnet:

This sonnet is divided into two parts.
In the first, I tell the cause why I abstain not
from coming to this lady.

In the 2nd,

→

I tell what befalls me through coming to her. And also this second part divides into five distinct statements. For, in the first, I say what Love, counseled by Reason, tells me when I am near the Lady.

> The thoughts are broken in my memory,
>   you lovely Joy, whenever I see your face;
>   when you are near me, Love fills up the space,
> often repeating, "If death irk you, fly."
> My face shows my heart's color, verily,
>   which, fainting, seeks for any leaning-place;
>   till, in the drunken terror of disgrace,
> the very stones seem to be shrieking, "Die!"
> It were a grievous sin, if one should not
>   strive then to comfort my bewildered mind
>   (though merely with a simple pitying)
> for the great anguish which your scorn has
>   wrought
>   in the dead sight of the eyes grown nearly blind,
>   which look for death as for a blessed thing.

In the second, I set forth the state of my heart by the example of the face. In the third, I say how all ground of trust fails me. In the fourth, I say that he sins who shows not pity of me, which would give me some comfort. In the last, I say why people should take pity; namely, for the piteous look which comes into mine eyes; which piteous look is destroyed, that is, appears not unto others, through the jeering of this lady, who draws to the like action those who peradventure would see this piteous. The second part begins here, "My face shows"; the third, "Till, in the drunken terror"; the fourth, "It were a grievous sin"; the fifth, "For the great anguish."

Thereafter, this sonnet bred in me desire to write down in verse four other things touching my condition, the which things it seemed to me that I had not yet made manifest. The first among these was the grief that possessed me very often, remembering the strangeness which Love wrought in me; the second was, how Love many times assailed me so suddenly and with such strength that I had no other life remaining except a thought which spoke of my lady; the third was, how when Love did battle with me in this wise, I would rise up all colorless, if so I might see my lady, conceiving that the sight of her would defend me against the assault of Love, and altogether forgetting that which her presence brought unto me; and the fourth was, how, when I saw her, the sight not only defended me not, but took away the little life that remained to me. And I said these four things in a sonnet, which is this:

> At whiles (yea oftentimes) I muse over
> > the quality of anguish that is mine
> > > through Love: then pity makes my voice to pine,
> saying, "Is any else thus, anywhere?"
> Love smites me, whose strength is ill to bear;
> > so that of all my life is left no sign
> > > except one thought; and that, because 'tis yours,
> leaves not the body but abides there.
> And then if I, whom other aid forsook,
> > would aid myself, and innocent of art
> > > would fain have sight of you as a last hope,
> no sooner do I lift my eyes to look
> > than the blood seems as shaken from my heart,
> > > and all my pulses beat at once and stop.

This sonnet is divided into four parts, four things being therein narrated; and as these are set forth above, I only proceed to distinguish the parts by their beginnings. Wherefore I say that the second part begins, "Love smites me"; the third, "And then if I"; the fourth "No sooner do I lift."

After I had written these three last sonnets, wherein I spoke unto my lady, telling her almost the whole of my condition, it seemed to me that I should be silent, having said enough concerning myself. But albeit I spoke not to her again, yet it behoved me afterward to write of another matter, more noble than the foregoing. And for that the occasion of what I then wrote may be found pleasant in the hearing, I will relate it as briefly as I may.

Through the sore change in my aspect, the secret of my heart was now understood of many. Which thing being thus, there came a day when certain ladies to whom it was well known (they having been with me at diverse times in my trouble) were met together for the pleasure of gentle company. And as I was going that way by chance (but I think rather by the will of fortune), I heard one of them call unto me, and she that called was a lady of very sweet speech. And when I had come close up with them, and perceived that they had not among them my excellent lady, I was reassured; and saluted them, asking of their pleasure. The ladies were many; diverse of whom were laughing one to another, while diverse gazed at me as though I should speak anon. But when I still spoke not, one of them, who before had been talking with another, addressed me by my name, saying, "To what end love you this lady, seeing that you can not support her presence? Now tell us this thing, that we may know it: for certainly the end of such a love must be worthy of knowledge." And when she had spoken these words, not she only, but all they that were with her, began to observe me, waiting for my reply. Whereupon I said unto them: "Ladies, the end and aim of my Love was but the salutation of that lady of whom I conceive that you are speaking; wherein alone I found that beatitude which is the goal of desire. And now that it has pleased her to deny me this, Love, my Master, of his great goodness has placed all my beatitude there where my hope will not fail me." Then those ladies began to talk closely together; and as I have seen snow fall among the rain, so was their talk mingled with sighs. But after a little, that lady who had been the first to address me, addressed me again in these words: "We pray you that you will tell us wherein abides this your beatitude." And answering, I said but thus much: "In those words that do praise my lady." To which she rejoined: "If your speech were true, those words that you did write concerning your condition would have been written with another intent."

Then I, being almost put to shame because of her answer, went out from among them; and as I walked, I said within myself: "Seeing that there is so much beatitude in those words which do praise my lady, wherefore has my speech of her been different?" And then I resolved that thenceforward I would choose for the theme of my writings only the praise of this most gracious being. But when I had thought exceedingly, it seemed to me that I had taken to myself a theme which was much too lofty, so that I dared not begin; and I remained during several days in the desire of speaking, and the fear of beginning. After which it happened, as I passed one day along a path which lay beside a stream of very clear water, that there came upon me a great desire to say somewhat in rhyme: but when I began thinking how I should say it, I thought that to speak of her was unseemly, unless I spoke to other ladies in the second person; which is to say, not to any other ladies, but only to such as are so called because they are gentle, let alone for mere womanhood. Whereupon I declare that my tongue spoke as though by its own impulse, and said, "Ladies that have intelligence in love." These words I laid up in my mind with great gladness, conceiving to take them as my commencement. Wherefore, having returned to the city I spoke of, and considered thereof during certain days, I began a poem with this beginning, constructed in the mode which will be seen below in its division. The poem begins here:

This poem, that it may be better understood, I will divide more subtly than the others preceding; and therefore I will make three parts of it. The first part is a proem to the words following. The second is the matter treated of. The third is, as it were, a handmaid to the preceding words. The second begins here, "An Angel"; the third here, "Dear Song, I know.' The first part is divided into four. In the first, I say to whom I mean to speak of my Lady, and wherefore I will so speak.
In the second, I say what she appears to myself to be when I reflect upon her excellence, and what I would utter if I lost not courage.

Ladies that have intelligence in love,
    of my own lady I would speak with you;
        not that I hope to count her praises through,
            but telling what I may, to ease my mind.
And I declare that when I speak thereof
Love sheds such perfect sweetness over me
that if my courage failed not, certainly
        to him my listeners must be all resigned.

        Wherefore I will not speak in such large kind
that my own speech should foil me, which were base;
but only will discourse of her high grace
        in these poor words, the best that I can find,
With you alone, dear dames and damozels:
'Twere ill to speak thereof with any else.

An Angel, of his blessed knowledge, says
    to God: "Lord, in the world that You have made,
        a miracle in action is displayed
            by reason of a soul whose splendors fare
even hither: and since Heaven requires
    nought saving her, for her it prays You,
        Your Saints crying aloud continually."
        Yet Pity still defends our earthly share
            in that sweet soul; God answering thus the prayer:

In the third, I say what it is I purpose to speak so as not to be impeded by faint-heartedness.

← In the fourth, repeating to whom I purpose speaking, I tell the reason why I speak to them.

← Then I begin treating of this lady: and this part is divided into two. In the first, I tell what is understood of her in heaven.

> *In the second, I tell what is understood of her on earth.*

"My well-beloved, suffer that in peace
your hope remain, while so My pleasure is,
 there where one dwells who dreads the loss of her:
and who in Hell unto the doomed shall say,
"I have looked on that for which God's chosen pray."

→

> *This second part is divided into two; for, in the first, I speak of her as regards the nobleness of her soul, relating some of her virtues proceeding from her soul.*

My lady is desired in the high Heaven:
wherefore, it now behoves me to tell,
saying: Let any maid that would be well
 esteemed keep with her: for as she goes by,
into foul hearts a deathly chill is driven
by Love, that makes ill thought to perish there:
while any who endured to gaze on her
 must either be ennobled, or else die.
When one deserving to be raised so high
is found, 'tis then her power attains its proof,
making his heart strong for his soul's behoof
 with the full strength of meek humility.
Also this virtue owns she, by God's will:
who speaks with her can never come to ill.

→

> *In the second, I speak of her as regards the nobleness*

Love says concerning her: "How chances it
 that flesh, which is of dust, should be thus pure?"
Then, gazing always, he makes oath: "Foresure,
 this is a creature of God till now unknown."

of her body, narrating some of her beauties. This second part is divided into two, for, in the first, I speak of certain beauties which belong to the whole person;< in the second, I speak of certain beauties which belong to a distinct part of the person. This second part is divided into two; for, in the one, I speak of the eyes, which are the beginning of love; in the second, I speak of the mouth, which is the end of love. And that every vicious thought may be discarded herefrom, let the reader remember that it is above written that the greeting of this lady, which was an act of her mouth, was the goal of my desires, while I could receive it.

Then, I add a stanza as it were handmaid to the others, wherein I say what I desire from this my poem. And because this last part is easy to understand, I trouble not myself with more divisions. I say, indeed, that the further to open the meaning of this poem, more minute divisions ought to be used; but nevertheless he who is not of wit enough to understand it by these which have been already made is welcome to leave it alone; for certes, I fear I have communicated its sense to too many by these present divisions, if it so happened that many should hear it.

> She has that paleness of the pearl that's fit
> in a fair woman, so much and not more:
> she is as high as Nature's skill can soar:
>   beauty is tried by her comparison.
>   Whatever her sweet eyes are turned upon,
> spirits of love do issue thence in flame,
> which through their eyes who then may look on them
>   pierce to the heart's deep chamber everyone.
> And in her smile Love's image you may see;
> whence none can gaze upon her steadfastly.
>
> Dear Song, I know you will hold gentle speech
> with many ladies, when I send you forth:
> wherefore (being mindful that you had your birth
>   from Love, and are a modest, simple child),
> whomso you meet, say you this to each:
> "Give me good speed! To her I wend along
> in whose much strength my weakness is
>   made strong."
>   And if, in the end, you would not be beguiled
>   of all your labor, seek not the defiled
> and common sort; but rather choose to be
> where man and woman dwell in courtesy.
>   So to the road you shall be reconciled,
> and find the lady, and with the lady, Love.
> Commend you me to each, as does behove.

When this song was a little gone abroad, a certain one of my friends, hearing the same, was pleased to question me, that I should tell him what thing love is; it may be, conceiving from the words thus heard, a hope of me beyond my desert. Wherefore I, thinking that after such discourse it were well to say somewhat of the nature of Love, and also in accordance with my friend's desire, proposed to myself to write certain words in which I should treat of this argument. And the sonnet that I then made is this:

> This sonnet is divided into two parts. In the first, I speak of him according to his power.

> Love and the gentle heart are one same thing,
> even as the wise man in his ditty says:
> each, of itself, would be such life in death
> as rational soul bereft of reasoning.
> 'Tis Nature makes them when she loves: a king
> Love is, whose palace where he sojourns
> is called the Heart; there draws he quiet breath
> at first, with brief or longer slumbering.
> Then beauty seen in virtuous womankind
> will make the eyes desire, and through the heart
>   send the desiring of the eyes again;
> where often it abides so long enshrined
>   that Love at length out of his sleep will start.
> And women feel the same for worthy me

In the second, I speak of him according as his power translates itself into act. The first is divided into two. In the first, I saw in what subject this power exists. In the second, I say how this subject and this power are produced together, and how the one regards the other, as form does matter.

    The second begins here, " 'Tis Nature." Afterwards when I say, "Then beauty seen in virtuous womankind," I say how this power translates itself into act; and, first, how it so translates itself in a man, when how it so translates itself in a woman: here, "And women feel."

Having treated of love in the foregoing, it appeared to me that I should also say something in praise of my lady, wherein it might be set forth how love manifested itself when produced by her; and how not only she could awaken it where it slept, but where it was not she could marvelously create it. To which end I wrote another sonnet; and it is this:

> My lady carries love within her eyes;
> all that she looks on is made pleasanter;
> upon her path men turn to gaze at her;
> he whom she greets feels his heart to rise,
> and droops his troubled visage, full of sighs,
> and of his evil heart is then aware:
> hate loves, and pride becomes a worshipper.
> O women, help to praise her in somewise.
> Humbleness, and the hope that hopeth well,
> by speech of hers into the mind are brought,
>   and who beholds is blessed oftenwhiles.
>   The look she has when she a little smiles
> cannot be said, nor holden in the thought;
> 'Tis such a new and gracious miracle.

This sonnet has three sections. In the first, I say how this lady brings this power into action by those most noble features, her eyes; and, in the third, I say this same as to that most noble feature, her mouth.

← And between these two sections in a little section, which asks, as it were, help for the previous section and the subsequent. The third begins here: "Humbleness." The first is divided into three; for, in the first, I say how she with power makes noble that which she is not. In the second, I say how she brings Love, in act, into the hearts of all those whom she sees. In the third, I tell what she afterwards, with virtue, operates upon their hearts. The second begins, "Upon her path"; the third, "He whom she greeteth." Then, when I say "O women, help," I intimate to whom it is my intention to speak, calling on women to help me to honor her. Then, when I say, "Humbleness," I say that same which is said in the first part, regarding two acts of her mouth, one whereof is her most sweet speech, and the other her marvelous smile. Only, I say not of this last how it operates upon the hearts of others, because memory cannot retain this smile, nor its operation.

Not many days after this (it being the will of the most High God, who also from Himself put not away death), the father of wonderful Beatrice, going out of this life, passed certainly into glory. Thereby it happened, as of very sooth it might not be otherwise, that this lady was made full of the bitterness of grief: seeing that such a parting is very grievous unto those friends who are left, and that no other friendship is like to that between a good parent and a good child; and furthermore considering that this lady was good in the supreme degree, and her father (as by many it has been truly averred) of exceeding goodness. And because it is the usage of that city that men meet with men in such a grief, and women with women, certain ladies of her companionship gathered themselves unto Beatrice, where she kept alone in her weeping: and as they passed in and out, I could hear them speak concerning her, how she wept. At length two of them went by me, who said: "Certainly she grieves in such sort that one might die for pity, beholding her." Then, feeling the tears upon my face, I put up my hands to hide them: and had it not been that I hoped to hear more concerning her (seeing that where I sat, her friends passed continually in and out), I should assuredly have gone thence to be alone, when I felt the tears come. But as I still sat in that place, certain ladies again passed near me, who were saying among themselves: "Which of us shall be joyful any more, who have listened to this lady in her piteous sorrow?" And there were others who said as they went by me: "He that sits here could not weep more if he had beheld her as we have beheld her"; and again: "He is so altered that he seems not as himself." And still as the ladies passed to and from, I could hear them speak after this fashion of her and of me.

Wherefore afterwards, having considered and perceiving that there was herein matter for poesy, I resolved that I would write certain rhymes in which should be contained all that those ladies had said. And because I would willingly have spoken to them if it had not been for discreetness, I made in my rhymes as though I had spoken and they had answered me.

And thereof I wrote two sonnets; in the first of which I addressed them as I would fain have done; and in the second related their answer, using the speech that I had heard from them, as though it had been spoken unto myself. And the sonnets are these:

This sonnet is divided into two parts. In the first, I call and ask these ladies whether they come from her, telling them that I think they do, because they return the nobler.

I

You that thus wear a modest countenance
   with lids weighed down by the heart's heaviness,
   whence come you, that among you every face
appears the same, for its pale troubled glance?
Have you beheld my lady's face, perchance,
   bowed with the grief that Love makes full of grace?
   Say now, "This thing is thus"; as my heart says,
marking your grace and sorrowful advance.
And if indeed you come from where she sighs
   and mourns, may it please you (for his heart's relief)
   to tell how it fares with her unto him
who knows that you have wept, seeing your eyes,
   and is so grieved with looking on your grief
     that his heart trembles and his sight grows dim?

In the second, I pray them to tell me of her.

This sonnet has four parts, as the ladies in whose person I reply had four forms of answer. And, because these are sufficiently shown above, I stay not to explain the purport of the parts, and therefore I only discriminate them.

II

The second begins here

Can you indeed be he that still would sing
of our dear lady unto none but us?
For though your voice confirms that it is thus,
your visage might another witness bring.
And wherefore is your grief so sore a thing
that grieving you make others dolorous?

the third here,

    Have you too seen her weep, that you from us
can not conceal your inward sorrowing?
Nay, leave our woe to us: let us alone

the fourth.

'twere sin if one should strive to soothe our woe,
    for in her weeping we have heard her speak:
also her look's so full of her heart's moan
that they who should behold her, looking so,
    must fall aswoon, feeling all life grow weak.

A few days after this, my body became afflicted with a painful infirmity, whereby I suffered bitter anguish for many days, which at last brought me unto such weakness that I could no longer move. And I remember that on the ninth day, being overcome with intolerable pain, a thought came into my mind concerning my lady: but when it had a little nourished this thought, my mind returned to its brooking over mine enfeebled body. And then perceiving how frail a thing life is, even though health keep with it, the matter seemed to me so pitiful that I could not choose but weep; and weeping I said within myself: "Certainly it must some time come to pass that the very gentle Beatrice will die." Then, feeling bewildered, I closed mine eyes; and my brain began to be in travail as the brain of one frantic, and to have such imaginations as here follow.

And at first, it seemed to me that I saw certain faces of women with their hair loosened, which called out to me, "You shall surely die"; after which, other terrible and unknown appearances said unto me, "You are dead." At length, as my phantasy held on in its wanderings, I came to be I knew not where, and to behold a throng of dishevelled ladies wonderfully sad, who kept going hither and thither weeping. Then the sun went out, so that the stars showed themselves, and they were of such a color that I knew they must be weeping: and it seemed to me that the birds fell dead out of the sky, and that there were great earthquakes. With that, while I wondered in my trance, and was filled with grievous fear, I conceived that a certain friend came unto me and said: "Have you not heard? She that was your excellent lady has been taken out of life." Then I began to weep very piteously; and not only in my imagination, but with my eyes, which were wet with tears. And I seemed to look towards Heaven, and to behold a multitude of angels who were returning upwards, having before them an exceedingly white cloud: and these angels were singing together gloriously, and the words of their song were these: "Osanna in excelis"; and there was no more that I heard. Then my heart that was so full of love said unto me: "It is true that our lady lies dead"; and it seemed to me that I went to look upon the body wherein that blessed and most noble spirit had had its abiding-place. And so strong was this idle imagining, that it made me to behold my lady in death, whose head certain ladies seemed to be covering with a white veil; and who was so humble of her aspect that it was as though she had said, "I have attained to look on the beginning of peace."

And therewithal I came unto such humility by the sight of her, that I cried out upon Death, saying: "Now come unto me, and be not bitter against me any longer: surely there where you have been, you have learned gentleness. Wherefore come now unto me who do greatly desire you: see you not that I wear your color already? And when I had seen all those offices performed that are fitting to be done unto the dead, it seemed to me that I went back unto my own chamber, and looked up towards Heaven. And so strong was my phantasy that I wept again in very truth, and said with my true voice: "O excellent soul! how blessed is he that now looks upon you!"

And as I said these words, with a painful anguish of sobbing and another prayer unto Death, a young and gentle lady, who had been standing beside me where I lay, conceiving that I wept and cried out because of the pain of my infirmity, was taken with trembling and began to shed tears. Whereby other ladies, who were about the room, becoming aware of my discomfort by reason of the moan that she made (who indeed was of my very near kindred), led her away from where I was, and then set themselves to awaken me, thinking that I dreamed, and saying: "Sleep no longer, and be not disquieted."

Then, by their words, this strong imagination was brought suddenly to an end, at the moment that I was about to say "O Beatrice! peace be with you." And already I had said, 'O Beatrice!" when being aroused, I opened my eyes, and knew that it had been a deception. But albeit I had indeed uttered her name, yet my voice was so broken with sobs, that it was not understood by these ladies; so that in spite of the sore shame that I felt, I turned towards them by Love's counseling. And when they beheld me, they began to say, "He seems as one dead," and to whisper among themselves, "Let us strive if we may not comfort him." Whereupon they spoke to me many soothing words, and questioned me moreover touching the cause of my fear. Then I, being somewhat reassured, and having perceived that it was a mere phantasy, said unto them, "This thing it was that made me afraid"; and told them of all that I had seen, from the beginning even unto the end, but without once speaking the name of my lady. Also, after I had recovered from my sickness, I bethought me to write these things in rhyme; deeming it a lovely thing to be known. Whereof I wrote this poem:

> This poem has two parts. In the first, speaking to a person undefined, I tell how I was aroused from a vain phantasy by certain ladies, and how I promised them to tell what it was. The first part divides into two. In the first, I tell that which certain ladies, and which one singly, did and said because of my phantasy, before I had returned into my right senses.
>
> In the second ➡ I tell what these ladies said to me after I had left off this wandering.

A very pitiful lady, very young,
exceeding rich in human sympathies,
    stood by, what time I clamored upon Death
and at the wild words wandering on my tongue
and at the piteous look within mine eyes
    she was affrighted, that sobs choked
    her breath.
    So by her weeping where I lay beneath,
some other gentle ladies came to know
my state, and made her go:
afterward, bending themselves over me,
one said, "Awaken you!"
    And one, "What thing your sleep disquiets?"
With that, my soul woke up from its eclipse,
the while my lady's name rose to my lips:
but uttered in a voice so sob-broken,
so feeble with the agony of tears
    that I alone might hear it in my heart;
and though that look was on my visage then
which he who is ashamed so plainly wears,
    Love made that I through shame held not apart,
    but gazed upon them. And my hue was such
that they looked at each other and thought of death;

saying under their breath
most tenderly, "O let us comfort him:"
then unto me: "What a dream
    was thine, that it has shaken you so much?"
And when I was a little comforted,
"This, ladies, was the dream I dreamt," I said.

"I was a-thinking how life fails with us
suddenly after such a little while;
    when Love sobbed in my heart, which is his home.
Whereby my spirit waxed so dolorous
that in myself I said, with sick recoil:
    "Yea, to my lady too this Death must come."
    And therewithal such a bewilderment
possessed me, that I shut mine eyes for peace;
and in my brain did cease
order of thought, and every healthful thing.
Afterwards, wandering
    amid a swarm of doubts that came and went,
some certain women's faces hurried by
and shrieked to me, "You too shall die, shall die!"

Then saw I many broken hinted sights
in the uncertain state I stepped into.
    Meseemed to be I know not in what place,
where ladies through the streets, like mournful
                                  lights,
ran with loose hair, and eyes that frightened you,
    by their own terror, and a pale amaze:
    the while, little by little, as I thought,
the sun ceased, and the stars began to gather,
and each wept at the other;
and the birds dropped in mid-flight out of the sky;

← In the second part, when I say, "I was a-thinking," I say how I told them this my imagination; and concerning this I have two parts. In the first, I tell, in order, this imagina--tion.

"Then lifting up mine eyes, as the tears came,
I saw the Angels, like a rain of manna,
    in a long flight flying back Heavenward;
having a little cloud in front of them,
after which they went and said, "Hosanna";
    and if they had said more, you should have heard.
    Then Love said, "Now shall all things be made
                                        clear:
come and behold our lady where she lies."
These 'wildering fantasies
then carried me to see my lady dead.
Even as I there was led,
    her ladies with a veil were covering her;
and with her was such a very humbleness
that she appeared to say, "I am at peace."

And I became so humble in my grief,
seeing in her such deep humility,
    that I said: "Death, I hold you passing good
henceforth, and a most gentle sweet relief,
since my dear love has chosen to dwell with thee:
pity, not hate, is yours, well understood.
    Lo! I do so desire to see your face
that I am like as one who nears the tomb;
my soul entreats you, Come."
Then I departed, having made my moan;
and when I was alone
    I said, and cast my eyes to the High Place:
"Blessed is he, fair soul, who meets your glance!"
…Just then you woke me, of your complaisaunce."

> In the second, → saying at what time they called me, I covertly thank them.

After this empty imagining, it happened on a day, as I sat thoughtful, that I was taken with such a strong trembling at the heart, that it could not have been otherwise in the presence of my lady. Whereupon I perceived that there was an appearance of Love beside me, and I seemed to see him coming from my lady; and he said, not aloud but within my heart: "Now take heed that you bless the day when I entered into you; for it is fitting that you should do so." And with that my heart was so full of gladness, that I could hardly believe it to be of very truth my own heart and not another.

A short while after these words which my heart spoke to me with the tongue of Love, I saw coming towards me a certain lady who was very famous for her beauty, and of whom that friend whom I have already called the first among my friends had long been enamoured. This lady's name was Joan; but because of her comeliness (or at least it was so imagined) she was called of many Primavera (Spring), and went by that name among them. Then looking again, I perceived that the most noble Beatrice followed after her. And when both these ladies had passed by me, it seemed to me that Love spoke again in my heart, saying: "She that came first was called Spring, only because of that which was to happen on this day. And it was I myself who caused this name to be given her; seeing that as the Spring comes first in the year, so should she come first on this day, when Beatrice was to show herself after the vision of her servant. And even if you go about to consider her right name, it is also as one should say, "She shall come first": inasmuch as her name, Joan, is taken from that John who went before the True Light, saying *Ego vox clamantis in deserto: Parate viam Domini* [I am the voice of one crying in the wilderness: "Prepare you the way of the Lord."] And also it seemed to me that he added other words, to wit: "He who should inquire delicately touching this matter, could not but call Beatrice by my own name, which is to say, Love; beholding her so like unto me."

Then I, having thought of this, imagined to write it with rhymes and send it unto my chief friend; but setting aside certain words which seemed proper to be set aside, because I believed that his heart still regarded the beauty of her that was called Spring. And I wrote this sonnet:

> This sonnet has many parts: whereof the first tells how I felt awakened within my heart the accustomed tremor, and how it seemed that Love appeared to me joyful from afar.

The second ➡ says how it appeared to me that Love spoke within my heart, and what was his aspect.

The third ➡ tells how, after he had in such wise been with me a space, I saw and heard certain things.

The third part divides into two. In the first, I say what I saw. In the second, I say what I heard.

> I felt a spirit of love begin to stir
> within my heart, long time unfelt till then;
> and saw Love coming towards me fair and fain
> (that I scarce knew him for his joyful cheer),
> saying, "Be now indeed my worshipper!"
> And in his speech he laughed and laughed again.
> Then, while it was his pleasure to remain,
> I chanced to look the way he had drawn near,
> and saw the Ladies Joan and Beatrice
> approach me, this the other following,
>   one and a second marvel instantly.
> And even as now my memory speaks this,
> Love spoke it then: "The first is christened
>   Spring;
>   the second Love, she is so like to me."

It might be here objected unto me, (and even by one worthy of controversy) that I have spoken of Love as though it were a thing outward and visible: not only a spiritual essence, but as a bodily substance also. The which thing, in absolute truth, is a fallacy; Love not being of itself a substance, but an accident of substance. Yet that I speak of Love as though it were a thing tangible and even human, appears by three things which I say thereof. And firstly, I say that I perceived Love coming towards me; whereby, seeing that to come bespeaks locomotion, and seeing also how philosophy teaches us that none but a corporeal substance has locomotion, it seems that I speak of Love as of a corporeal substance. And secondly, I say that Love smiled: and thirdly, that Love spoke; faculties (and especially the risible faculty) which appear proper unto humans: whereby it further seems that I speak of Love as of human. Now that this matter may be explained, (as is fitting) it must first be remembered that anciently they who wrote poems of Love wrote not in the vulgar tongue, but rather certain poets in the Latin tongue. I mean, among us, although perchance the same may have been among others, and although likewise, as among the Greeks, they were not writers of spoken language, but men of letters treated of these things. And indeed it is not a great number of years since poetry began to be made in the vulgar tongue; the writing of rhymes in spoken language corresponding to the writing in meter of Latin verse, by a certain analogy. And I say that it is but a little while, because if we examine the language of *oco* [Provençal] and the language of *si* [Tuscan], we shall not find in those tongues any written thing of an earlier date than the last hundred and fifty years. Also the reason why certain of a very mean sort obtained at the first some fame as poets is, that before then no one has written verses in the language of si: and of these, the first was moved to the writing of such verses by the wish to make himself understood of a certain lady, unto whom Latin poetry was difficult. This thing is against such as rhyme concerning other matters than love; that mode of speech having been first used for the expression of love alone. Wherefore, seeing that poets have a license allowed them that is not allowed unto the writers of prose, and seeing also that they who write in rhyme are simply poets in the vulgar tongue, it becomes fitting and reasonable that a larger license should be given to these than to other modern writers; and that any metaphor or rhetorical similitude which is permitted unto poets, should also be counted not unseemly in the rhymers of the vulgar tongue. This, if we perceive that the former have caused inanimate things to speak as though they had sense and reason, and to discourse one with another; yea, and not only actual things, but such also as have no real existence (seeing that they have made things which are not, to speak; and oftentimes written of those which are merely accidents as though they were substances and things human); it should therefore be permitted to the latter to do the like; which is to say, not inconsiderately, but with such sufficient motive as may afterwards be set forth in prose.

That the Latin poets have done thus, appears through Virgil, where he says that Juno (to wit, a goddess hostile to the Trojans) spoke unto Aeolus, master of the Winds; as it is written in the first book of the Aeneid, Aeole, *namque tibi*, &c.; and that this master of the Winds made reply: *Tuus, o regino, quid optes—Explorare labor, mihi jussa capessere fas est*. And through the same poet, the inanimate thing speaks unto the animate, in the third book of the Aeneid, where it is written: *Dardanidoe duri*, &c. With Lucan, the animate thing speaks to the inanimate; as thus: *Multun, Roma, tamen debes civilibus armis*. In Horace, one is made to speak to his own intelligence as unto another person; (and not only has Horace done this, but herein he follows the excellent Homer) as thus in his *Poetics; Dic mihi, Musa, virum*, &c. Through Ovid, Love speaks as a human creature, in the beginning of his discourse De Remediis Amoris: as thus: *Bella mihi, video, bello parantur, ait*. By which ensamples this thing shall be made manifest unto such as may be offended at any part of this my book. And lest some of the common sort should be moved to jeering hereat, I will here add, that neither did these ancient poets speak thus without consideration, nor should they who are makers of rhyme in our day write after the same fashion, having no reason in what they write; for it were a shameful thing if one should rhyme under the semblance of metaphor or rhetorical similitude, and afterwards, being questioned thereof, should be unable to rid his words of such semblance, unto their right understanding. Of whom (to wit, of such as rhyme thus foolishly), myself and the first among my friends do know many.

But returning to the matter of my discourse. This excellent lady of whom I spoke in what has gone before, came at last into such favor with all people, that when she passed anywhere folk ran to behold her; which thing was a deep joy to me: and when she drew near unto any, so much truth and simpleness entered into his heart, that he dared neither to lift his eyes nor to return her salutation: and unto this, many who have felt it can bear witness. She went along crowned and clothed with humility, showing no whit of pride in all that she heard and saw: and when she had gone by, it was said of many, "This is not a woman, but one of the beautiful angels of Heaven"; and there were some that said: "This is surely a miracle; blessed be the Lord, who has power to work thus marvellously." I say, of very sooth, that she showed herself so gentle and so full of all perfection, that she bred in those who looked upon her a soothing quiet beyond any speech; neither could any look upon her without sighing immediately. These things, and things yet more wonderful, were brought to pass through her miraculous virtue. Wherefore I, considering thereof and wishing to resume the endless tale of her praises, resolved to write somewhat wherein I might dwell on her surpassing influence; to the end that not only they who had beheld her, but others also, might know as much concerning her as words could give to the understanding. And it was then that I wrote this sonnet:

> My lady looks so gentle and so pure
> when yielding salutation by the way
> that the tongue trembles and has nought to say,
> and the eyes, which fain would see, may not endure.
> And still, amid the praise she hears secure,
> she walks with humbleness for her array;
> seeming a creature sent from Heaven to stay
> on earth, and show a miracle made sure.
> She is so pleasant in the eyes of men
> that through the sight the inmost heart does gain
> a sweetness which needs proof to know it by:
> and from between her lips there seems to move
> a soothing essence that is full of love
> saying forever to the spirit, "Sigh!"

This sonnet is so easy to understand, from what is afore narrated, that it needs no division; and therefore, leaving it, I say also that this excellent lady came into such favor with all people, that not only she herself was honored and commended, but through her companionship, honor and commendation came unto others. Wherefore I, perceiving this, and wishing that it should also be made manifest to those that beheld it not, wrote the sonnet here following; wherein is signified the power which her virtue had upon other ladies:

This sonnet has three parts. In the first, I say in what company this lady appeared most wondrous.

> For certain he has seen all perfectness
> who among other ladies has seen mine:
> they that go with her humbly should combine
> to thank their God for such peculiar grace.
> So perfect is the beauty of her face
> that it begets in no wise any sign
> of envy, but draws round her a clear line
> of love, and blesed faith, and gentleness.
> Merely the sight of her makes all things bow:
> not she herself alone is holier
>   than all; but hers, through her, are raised
>   above.
> From all her acts such lovely graces flow
> that truly one may never think of her
>   without a passion of exceeding love.

← In the second, I say how gracious was her society.

← In the third, I tell of the things which she, with power, worked upon others. This last part divides into three. In the first, I tell what she operated upon women, that is, by their own faculties. In the second, I tell what she operated in them through others.

In the third, I say how she not only operated in women, but in all people; and not only while herself present, but, by memory of her, operated wondrously.

Thereafter on a day, I began to consider that which I had said of my lady: to wit, in these two sonnets aforegone: and becoming aware that I had not spoken of her immediate effect on me at that especial time, it seemed to me that I had spoken defectively. Whereupon I resolved to write somewhat of the manner wherein I was then subject to her influence, and of what her influence then was. And conceiving that I should not be able to say these things in the small compass of a sonnet, I began therefore a poem with this beginning:

> Love has so long possessed me for his own
>   And made his lordship so familiar
> That he, who at first irked me, is now grown
>   Unto my heart as its best secrets are.
>   And thus, when he in such sore wise doth mar
> My life that all its strength seems gone from it,
> Mine inmost being then feels thoroughly quit
>   Of anguish, and all evil keeps afar.
> Love also gathers to such power in me
>   That my sighs speak, each one a grievous thing,
>   Always soliciting
> My lady's salutation piteously.
> Whenever she beholds me, it is so,
> Who is more sweet than any words can show.

Quomodo sedet sola civitas plena populo! facta est quasi vidua domina gentium! [How does the city sit solitary, that was full of people! how is she become as a widow, she that was great among the nations!—*Lamentations of Jeremiah*, i.1]
I was still occupied with this poem (having composed thereof only the above written stanza), when the Lord God of justice called my most gracious lady unto Himself, that she might be glorious under the banner of that blessed Queen Mary, whose name had always a deep reverence in the words of holy Beatrice. And because haply it might be found good that I should say somewhat concerning her departure, I will herein declare what are the reasons which made that I shall not do so.

    And the reasons are three. The first is such matter belongs not of right to the present argument; if one consider the opening of this little book. The second is, that even though the present argument required it, my pen does not suffice to write in a fit manner of this thing. And the third is, that were it both possible and absolute necessity, it would still be unseemly for me to speak thereof, seeing that thereby it must behove me to speak also my own praises: a thing that in whosoever does it is worthy of blame. For which reasons, I will leave this matter to be treated of by some other than myself.

Nevertheless, as the number nine, which number has often had mention in what has gone before (and not, as it might appear, without reason), seems also to have borne a part in the manner of her death: it is therefore right that I should say somewhat thereof. And for this cause, having first said what was the part it bore herein, I will afterwards point out a reason which made that this number was so closely allied unto my lady.

I say, then, that according to the division of time in Italy her most noble spirit departed from among us in the first hour of the ninth day of the month; and according to the division of time in Syria, in the ninth month of the year: seeing that Tismim, which with us is October, is there the first month. Also she was taken from among us in that year of our reckoning (to wit, of the years of our Lord) in which the perfect number was nine times multiplied within that century wherein she was born to this world: which is to say, the thirteenth century of Christians. [Beatrice Portinari will thus be found to have died during the first hour of the 9th of June, 1290.]

And touching the reason why this number was so closely allied unto her, it may peradventure be this. According to Ptolemy (and also to the Christian verity), the revolving heavens are nine; and according to the common opinion among astrologers, these nine heavens together have influence over the earth. Wherefore it would appear that this number was thus allied unto her for the purpose of signifying that, at her birth, all these nine heavens were at perfect unity with each other as to their influence. This is one reason that may be brought:

but more narrowly considering, and according to the infallible truth, this number was her own self: that is to say, by similitude. As thus. The number three is the root of the number nine; seeing that without the interposition of any other number, being multiplied merely by itself, it produces nine, as we manifestly perceive that three times three are nine. Thus, three being of itself the efficient of nine, and the Great Efficient of Miracles being of Himself Three Persons (to wit: the Father, the Son, and the Holy Spirit), which being Three, are also One:—this lady was accompanied by the number nine to the end that men might clearly perceive her to be a nine, that is, a miracle, whose only root is the Holy Trinity. It may be that a more subtle person would find for this thing a reason of greater subtilty: but such is the reason that I find, and that likes me best.

After this most gracious creature had gone out from among us, the whole city came to be as it were widowed and despoiled of all dignity. Then I, left mourning in this desolate city, wrote unto the principal persons thereof, in an epistle, concerning its condition; taking for my commencement those words of Jeremias: *Quomodo sedet sola civitas!* [How does the city sit solitary] &c. And I make mention of this, that none may marvel wherefore I set down these words before, in beginning to treat of her death. Also if any should blame me, in that I do not transcribe that epistle whereof I have spoken, I will make it my excuse that I began this little book with the intent that it should be written altogether in the vulgar tongue; wherefore, seeing that the epistle I speak of is in Latin, it belongs not to my understanding: more especially as I know that my chief friend, for whom I write this book, wished also that the whole of it should be in the vulgar tongue.

When my eyes had wept for some while, until they were so weary with weeping that I could no longer through them give ease to my sorrow, I bethought me that a few mournful words might stand me instead of tears. And therefore I proposed to make a poem, that weeping I might speak therein of her for whom so much sorrow had destroyed my spirit; and I then began "The eyes that weep."

This poor little poem has three parts. The first is a prelude. In the second, I speak of her. In the third, I speak pitifully to the poem. The first divides into three. In the first, I say what moves me to speak.

The eyes that weep for pity of the heart
have wept so long that their grief languishes,
    and they have no more tears to weep withal:
and now, if I would ease me of a part
of what, little by little, leads to death,
    it must be done by speech, or not at all.
    And because often, thinking, I recall
how it was pleasant, ere she went afar,
to talk of her with you, kind damozels,
I talk with no one else,
but only with such hearts as women's are.

In the second, ➡ I say to whom I mean to speak.

And I will say—still sobbing as speech fails—
that she has gone to Heaven suddenly,
and has left Love below, to mourn with me.

In the third ➡ I say of whom I mean to speak.

Then, when I say, ➡ "Beatrice is gone up," I speak of her; and concerning this I have two parts. First, I tell the cause why she was taken away from us:

Beatrice is gone up into high Heaven,
the kingdom where the angels are at peace;
    and lives with them: and to her friends
    is dead.
not by the frost of winter was she driven
away, like others; nor by summer-heats;
    but through a perfect gentleness, instead.
    For from the lamp of her meek lowlihead
such an exceeding glory went up hence
that it woke wonder in the Eternal Sire,
until a sweet desire
entered Him for that lovely excellence,
so that He bade her to Himself aspire;

counting this weary and most evil place
unworthy of a thing so full of grace.
Wonderfully out of the beautiful form
soared her clear spirit, waxing glad the while;
    and is in its first home, there where it is.
Who speaks thereof, and feels not the tears warm
upon his face, must have become so vile
    as to be dead to all sweet sympathies.

⬅ Afterwards, I say how one weeps her parting. This part divides into three. In the first, I say who it is that weeps her not.

    Out upon him! an abject wretch like this
may not imagine anything of her—
he needs no bitter tears for his relief.
But sighing comes, and grief,
and the desire to find no comforter
(save only Death, who makes all sorrow brief),
to him who for a while turns in hus thought
How she has been among us, and is not.

⬅ In the second, I say who it is that does weep her.

With sighs my bosom always labors
iin thinking, as I do continually,
   of her for whom my heart now breaks apace;
and very often when I think of death,
such a great inward longing comes to me
    that it will change the color of my face;
    and, if the idea settles in its place
all my limbs shake as with an ague-fit:
    till, starting up in wild bewilderment,
    I do become so shent
that I go forth, lest folk misdoubt of it.
    Afterward, calling with a sore lament
on Beatrice, I ask, "Can you be dead?"
and calling on her, I am comforted.

⬅ In the third, I speak of my condition.

Grief with its tears, and anguish with its sighs,
come to me now whenever I am alone;
    so that I think the sight of me gives pain.
And what my life has been, that living dies,
since for my lady the New Birth's begun,
    I have not any language to explain.
    And so, dear ladies, though my heart were fain,
I scarce could tell indeed how I am thus.
All joy is with my bitter life at war;
yea, I am fallen so far
that all men seem to say, "Go out from us,"
eyeing my cold white lips, how dead they are.
But she, though I be bowed unto the dust,
watches me; and will guerdon me, I trust.

Then, when I say, "Weep, pitiful Song of mine," I speak to this my song, telling it what ladies go to, and stay with. ➜

Weep, pitiful Song of mine, upon your way,
to the dames going and the damozels
for whom and for none else
your sisters have made music many a day.
You, that are very sad and not as they
go dwell you with them as a mourner dwells.

After I had written this poem, I received the visit of a friend whom I counted as second unto me in the degrees of friendship, and who, moreover, had been united by the nearest kindred to that most gracious creature. And when we had a little spoken together, he began to solicit me that I would write somewhat in memory of a lady who had died; and he disguised his speech, so as to seem to be speaking of another who was but lately dead: wherefore I, perceiving that his speech was of none other than that blessed one herself, told him that it should be done as he required. Then afterwards, having thought thereof, I imagined to give vent in a sonnet to some part of my hidden lamentations; but in such sort that it might seem to be spoken by this friend of mine, to whom I was to give it. And the sonnet says thus: "Stay now with me," etc.

Stay now with me, and listen to my sighs,
you piteous hearts, as pity bids you do.
Mark how they force their way out and
    press through:
if they be once pent up, the whole life dies.
Seeing that now indeed my weary eyes
oftener refuse than I can tell to you
(even though my endless grief is ever new),
to weep and let the smothered anguish rise.
Also in sighing you shall hear me call
on her whose blessed presence does enrich
    the only home that well befitted her:
And you shall hear a bitter scorn of all
sent from the inmost of my spirit in speech
    that mourns its joy and its joy's minister.

This sonnet has two parts. In the first, I call the Faithful of Love to hear me.

← In the 2nd, I relate my miserable condition.

But when I had written this sonnet, bethinking me who he was to whom I was to give it, that it might appear to be his speech, it seemed to me that this was a poor and barren gift for one of her so near kindred. Wherefore, before giving him this sonnet, I wrote two stanzas of a poem: the first being written in very sooth as though it were spoken by him, but the other being my own speech, albeit, unto one who should not look closely, they would both seem to be said by the same person. Nevertheless, looking closely, one must perceive that it is not so, inasmuch as one does not call this most gracious creature his lady, and the other does, as is manifestly apparent. And I gave the poem and the sonnet unto my friend, saying that I had made them only for him.

Whatever while the thought comes over me
that I may not again
    behold that lady whom I mourn
    for now,
about my heart my mind brings constantly
so much of extreme pain
    that I say, Soul of mine, why stay you?
    Truly the anguish, soul, that we must bow
beneath, until we win out of this life,
gives me full oft a fear that trembles:
so that I call on Death
even as on Sleep one calls after strife,
saying, Come unto me. Life shows grim
and bare; and if one dies, I envy him.

Forever, among all my sighs which burn,
there is a piteous speech
    that clamors upon death continually:
yea, unto him does my whole spirit turn
since first his hand did reach
    my lady's life with most foul cruelty.
    But from the height of woman's
        fairness, she,
going up from us with the joy we had,
grew perfectly and spiritually fair;
that so she spreads even there
a light of Love which makes the Angels glad,
and even unto their subtle minds can bring
a certain awe of profound marvelling.

The poem begins, "Whatever while," and has two parts. In the first, that is, in the first stanza, this my dear friend, her kinsman, laments.

← In the second, I lament. And thus it appears that in this poem two persons lament, of whom one laments as a brother, the other as a servant.

On that day which fulfilled the year since my lady had been made of the citizens of eternal life, remembering me of her as I sat alone, I betook myself to draw the resemblance of an angel upon certain tablets. And while I did thus, chancing to turn my head, I perceived that some were standing beside me to whom I should have given courteous welcome, and that they wre observing what I did: also I learned afterwards that they had been there a while before I perceived them. Perceiving whom, I arose for salutation, and said: "Another was with me."

Afterwards, when they had left me, I set myself again to my occupation, to wit, to the drawing figures of angels: in doing which, I conceived to write of this matter in rhyme, as for her anniversary, and to address my rhymes unto those who had just left me. It was then that I wrote the sonnet which says "That lady": and as this sonnet has two commencements, it behoveth me to divide it with both of them here.

That lady of all gentle memories
had lighted on my soul—whose new abode
lies now, as it was well ordained of God,
among the poor in heart, where Mary is.
Love, knowing that dear image to be his,
woke up within the sick heart sorrow-bowed,
unto the sights which are its weary load
saying, "Go forth." And they went forth, I wis;
forth went they from my breast that
   throbbed and ached;
with such a pang as oftentimes will bathe
   my eyes with tears when I am left alone.
And still those sighs which drew the heaviest
       breath
came whispering thus: "O noble intellect!
   It is a year today that you are gone!"

SECOND BEGINNING

That lady of all gentle memories
had lighted on my soul—for whose sake flowed
the tears of Love; in whom the power abode
which led you to observe while I did this.
Love, knowing that dear image to be his, &c.

I say that, according to the first commencement, this sonnet has three parts. In the first, I say that this lady was then in my memory.

← In the second, I tell what Love therefore did with me.

← In the third, I speak of the effects of Love. This part divides into two. In the other, I say how some spoke certain words different from the others.

← The second begins here. In this same manner is it divided with the other beginning, save that, in the first part, I tell when this lady had thus come into my mind, and this I say not in the other.

Then, having sat for some space sorely in thought because of the time that was now past, I was so filled with dolorous imaginings that it became outwardly manifest in my altered countenance. Whereupon, feeling this and being in dread lest any should have seen me, I lifted my eyes to look; and then perceived a young and very beautiful lady, who was gazing upon me from a window with a gaze full of pity so that the very sum of pity appeared gathered together in her. And seeing that unhappy persons, when they beget compassion in others, are then most moved unto weeping, as though they also felt pity for themselves, it came to pass that my eyes began to be inclined unto tears. Wherefore, becoming fearful lest I should make manifest my abject condition, I rose up, and went where I could not be seen of that lady; saying afterwards within myself: "Certainly with her also must abide most noble Love." And with that, I resolved upon writing a sonnet, wherein, speaking unto her, I should say all that I have just said. And as this sonnet is very evident, I will not divide it:

> My eyes beheld the blessed pity spring
> into your countenance immediately
> a while agone, when you beheld in me
> the sickness only hidden grief can bring;
> and then I knew you were considering
> how abject and forlorn my life must be;
> and I became afraid that you should see
> my weeping, and account it a base thing.
> Therefore I went out from you: feeling how
> the tears were straightway loosened at my heart
>   beneath your eyes' compassionate control.
>   And afterwards I said within my soul:
> "Lo! with this lady dwells the counterpart
> of the same Love who holds me weeping now."

It happened after this that whensoever I was seen of this lady, she became pale and of a piteous countenance, as though it had been with love; whereby she remembered me many times of my own most noble lady, who was wont to be of a like paleness. And I know that oftevn, when I could not weep nor in any way give ease unto my anguish, I went to look upon this lady, who seemed to bring the tears into my eyes by the mere sight of her. Of which thing I bethought me to speak unto her in rhyme, and then made this sonnet:

> Love's pallor and the semblance of deep ruth
> were never yet shown forth so perfectly
> in any lady's face, chancing to see
> grief's miserable countenance uncouth,
> as in yours, lady, they have sprung to soothe,
> when in my anguish you have looked on me;
> until sometimes it seems as if, through you,
> my heart might almost wander from its truth.
> Yet so it is, I cannot hold my eyes
> from gazing very often upon yours
>   in the sore hope to shed those tears they keep;
> and at such time, you make the pent tears rise
> even to the brim, till the eyes waste and pine;
>   yet cannot they, while you are present, weep.

At length, by the constant sight of this lady, my eyes began to be gladdened overmuch with her company; through which thing many times I had much unrest, and rebuked myself as a base person: also, many times I cursed the unsteadfastness of my eyes, and said to them inwardly: "Was not your grievous condition of weeping wont one while to make others weep? And will ye now forget this thing because a lady looks upon you? who so looks merely in compassion of the grief you then showed for your own blessed lady. But whatso you can, do you, accursed eyes! many a time will I make you remember it! for never, till death dry you up, should you make an end of your weeping." And when I had spoken thus unto my eyes, I was taken again with extreme and grievous sighing. And to the end that this inward strife which I had undergone might not be hidden from all saving the miserable wretch who endured it, I proposed to write a sonnet, and to comprehend in it this horrible condition. And I wrote this which begins, "The very bitter weeping."

"The very bitter weeping that you made
so long a time together, eyes of mine,
was wont to make the tears of pity shine
in other eyes full oft, as I have said.
But now this thing were scarce remembered
if I, on my part, foully would combine
with you, and not recall each ancient sign
of grief, and her for whom your tears were shed.
It is your fickleness that does betray
my mind to fears and makes me tremble thus
    what while a lady greets me with her eyes.
except by death, we must not any way
forget our lady who is gone from us."
    So far does my heart utter, and then sighs.

The sonnet has two parts. In the first, I speak to my eyes, as my heart spoke within myself.

In the second, I remove a difficulty, showing who it is that speaks thus. It well might receive other divisions also; but this would be useless, since it is manifest by the preceding exposition.

The sight of this lady brought me into so unwonted a condition that I often thought of her as of one too dear unto me; and I began to consider her thus: "This lady is young, beautiful, gentle, and wise: perchance it was Love himself who set her in my path, that so my life might find peace." And there were times when I thought yet more fondly, until my heart consented unto its reasoning. But when it had so consented, my thought would often turn round upon me, as moved by reason, and cause me to say within myself: "What hope is this which would console me after so base a fashion, and which has taken the place of all other imagining?" Also there was another voice within me, that said: "And will you, having suffered so much tribulation through Love, not escape while yet you may from so much bitterness? You must surely know that this thought carries with it the desire of Love, and drew its life from the gentle eyes of that lady who vouchsafed you so much pity." Wherefore I, having striven sorely and very often with myself, bethought me to say somewhat thereof in rhyme. And seeing that in the battle of doubts, the victory most often remained with such as inclined towards the lady of whom I speak, it seemed to me that I should address this sonnet unto her: in the first line whereof, I call that thought which spoke of her a gentle thought, only because it spoke of one who was gentle; being of itself most vile.

In this sonnet I make myself into two, according as my thoughts were divided one from the other. The one part I call Heart, that is, appetite; the other, Soul, that is, reason; and I tell what one said to the other. And that it is fitting to call the appetite Heart, and the reason Soul, is manifest enough to them to whom I wish this to be open. True it is that, in the preceding sonnet, I take the part of the Heart against the Eyes; and that appears contrary to what I say in the present; and therefore I say that, there also, by the Heart I mean appetite, because yet greater was my desire to remember my most gentle lady than to see this other, although indeed I had some appetite towards her, but it appeared slight: wherefrom it appears that the one statement is not contrary to the other.

> A gentle thought there is will often start,
> within my secret self, to speech of you:
> also of Love it speaks so tenderly
> that much in me consents and takes its part.
> "And what is this," the soul says to the heart,
> "that comes thus to comfort you and me,
> and thence where it would dwell, thus potently
> can drive all other thoughts by its strange art?"
> And the heart answers: "Be no more at strife
> 'twixt doubt and doubt: this is Love's messenger
>   and speaks but his words, from him received;
> and all the strength it owns and all the life
> it draws from the gentle eyes of her
>   who, looking on our grief, has often grieved."

This sonnet has three parts. In the first, I begin to say to this lady how my desires turn all toward her.

← In the second, I say how the Soul, that is the reason, speaks to the Heart, that is, to the appetite.

← In the third, I say how the latter answers.

But against this adversary of reason, there rose up in me on a certain day, about the ninth hour, a strong visible fantasy, wherein I seemed to behold the most gracious Beatrice, habited in that crimson raiment which she had worn when I had first beheld her; also she appeared to me of the same tender age as then. Whereupon I fell into a deep thought of her: and my memory ran back, according to the order of time, unto all those matters in which she had borne a part; and my heart began painfully to repent of the desire by which it had basely let itself be possessed during so many days, contrary to the constancy of reason.

And then, this evil desire being quite gone from me, all my thoughts turned again unto their excellent Beatrice. And I say most truly that from that hour I thought constantly of her with the whole humbled and ashamed heart; which became often manifest in sighs, that had among them the name of that most gracious creature, and how she departed from us. Also it would come to pass very often, through the bitter anguish of some one thought, that I forgot both it, and myself, and where I was. By this increase of sights, my weeping, which before had been somewhat lessened, increased in like manner; so that my eyes seemed to long only for tears and to cherish them, and came at last to be circled about with red as though they had suffered martrydom: neither were they able to look again upon the beauty of any face that might again bring them to shame and evil: from which things it will appear that they were fitly guerdoned for their unsteadfastness. Wherefore I (wishing that my abandonment of all such evil desires and vain temptations should be certified and made manifest, beyond all doubts which might have been suggested by the rhymes aforewritten) proposed to write a sonnet wherein I should express this purport. And I then wrote, "Woe's me!"

I said, "Woe's me!" because I was ashamed of the trifling of my eyes. This sonnet I do not divide, since its purport is manifest enough.

> Woe's me! by dint of all these sighs that come
> forth of my heart, its endless grief to prove,
> my eyes are conquered, so that even to move
> their lids for greeting is grown troublesome.
> They wept so long that now they are grief's home
> and count their tears all laughter far above;
> they wept till they are circled now by Love
> with a red circle in sign of martyrdom.
> These musings, and the sighs they bring from me,
> are grown at last so constant and so sore
>   that love swoons in my spirit with faint breath;
> hearing in those sad sounds continually
> the most sweet name that my dead lady bore,
>   with many grievous words touching her death.

About this time, it happened that a great number of persons undertook a pilgrimage, to the end that they might behold that blessed portraiture bequeathed unto us by our Lord Jesus Christ as the image of His beautiful countenance (upon which countenance my dear lady now looketh continually). And certain among these pilgrims, who seemed very thoughtful, passed by a path which is well-nigh in the midst of the city where my most gracious lady was born, and abode, and at last died.

Then I, beholding them, said within myself: "These pilgrims seem to be come from very far; and I think they cannot have heard speak of this lady, or know anything concerning her. Their thoughts are not of her, but of other things; it may be, of their friends who are far distant, and whom we, in our turn, know not." And I went on to say: "I know that if they were of a country near unto us, they would in some wise seem disturbed, passing through this city which is so full of grief." And I said also: "If I could speak with them a space, I am certain that I should make them weep before they went forth of this city; for those things that they would hear from me must needs beget weeping in any."

And when the last of them had gone by me, I bethought me to write a sonnet, showing forth my inward speech; and that it might seem the more pitiful, I made as though I had spoken it indeed unto them. And I wrote this sonnet, which begins: "You pilgrim-folk." I made use of the word pilgrim for its general signification; for "pilgrim" may be understood in two senses, one general, and one special. General, so far as any one may be called a pilgrim who leaves the place of his birth; whereas, more narrowly speaking, he only is a pilgrim who goeth towards or frowards the House of St. James. For there are three separate denominations proper unto those who undertake journeys to the glory of God. They are called Palmers who go beyond the seas eastward, whence often they bring palm-branches. And Pilgrims, as I have said, are they who journey unto the holy House of Galicia; seeing that no other apostle was buried so far from his birth-place as was the blessed Saint James. And there is a third sort who are called Romers; in that they go whither these whom I have called pilgrims went: which is to say, unto Rome.

This sonnet is not divided, because its own words sufficiently declare it.

> You pilgrim-folk, advancing pensively
>   as if in thought of distant things, I pray,
>   is your own land indeed so far away—
> as by your aspect it would seem to be—
> that this our heavy sorrow leaves you free
>   though passing through the mournful town midway;
>   like unto men that understand today
> nothing at all of her great misery?
> Yet if you will but stay, whom I accost,
>   and listen to my words a little space,
>   at going you shall mourn with a loud voice.
> It is her Beatrice that she has lost;
>   of whom the least word spoken holds such grace
>   that men weep hearing it, and have no choice.

A while after these things, two gentle ladies sent unto me, praying that I would bestow upon them certain of these my rhymes. And I (taking into account their worthiness and consideration), resolved that I would write also a new thing, and send it them together with those others, to the end that their wishes might be honorably fulfilled. Therefore I made a sonnet, which narrates my condition, and which I caused to be conveyed to them, accompanied by the one preceding, and with that other which begins, "Stay now with me and listen to my sighs." And the new sonnet is, "Beyond the sphere."

This sonnet comprises five parts. In the first, I tell whither my thought goes, naming the place by the name of one of its effects. In the second, I say wherefore it goes up and who makes it go thus. ➔ In the third, ➔ I tell what it saw, namely, a lady honored. And I then call it a "Pilgrim Spirit," because it goes up spiritually, and like a pilgrim who is out of his known country.

> Beyond the sphere which spreads to widest space
>   now soars the sigh that my heart sends above;
> a new perception born of grieving Love
>   guides it upward the trodden ways.
> When it has reached unto the end, and stays,
>   it sees a lady round whom splendors move
> in homage; till, by the great light thereof
>   abashed, the pilgrim spirit stands at gaze.
> It sees her such, that when it tells me this
>   which it has seen, I understand it not,
> it has a speech so subtle and so fine.
> And yet I know its voice within my thought
>   often remembered me of Beatrice:
> so that I understand it, ladies mine.

In the fourth, I say how the spirit sees her such (that is, in such quality) that I cannot understand her; that is to say my thought rises into the quality of her in a degree that my intellect cannot comprehend, seeing that our intellect is, towards those blessed souls, like our eye weak against the suns; and this the Philosopher says in the Second of the Metaphysics. In the fifth, "And yet I know," I say that, although I cannot see there whither my thought carries me— that is, to her admirable essence—I at least understand this, namely, that it is a thought of my lady, because I often hear her name therein. And, at the end of this fifth part, I say, "Ladies mine," to say that they are ladies to whom I speak. It might be divided yet more nicely, and made yet clearer; but this division may pass, and therefore I stay not to divide it further.

After writing this sonnet, it was given to me to behold a very wonderful vision: in which I saw things which determined me to say nothing further of this most blessed one, until such time as I could discourse more worthily concerning her. And to this end I labor all I can: as she well knows. Wherefore if it be His pleasure through whom is the life of all things, that my life continue a few years, it is my hope that I shall yet write concerning her what has not before been written of any woman. After which, may it seem good to Him who is the Master of Grace, that my spirit should go there to behold the glory of its lady: that is, of that blessed Beatrice who now gazes continually on His countenance *qui est per omnia saecula benedictus* [Who is blessed throughout all ages]. *Laus Deo.*

THE END OF THE NEW LIFE

Works

Beatrice's Death and After

DANTE ALIGHIERI
Sonnet: On the 9th of June 1290

Upon a day, came Sorrow in to me,
    saying, "I've come to stay with you a while";
    and I perceived that she had ushered Bile
and Pain into my house for company.
Wherefore I said, "Go forth—away with you!"
    But like a Greek she answered, full of guile,
    and went on arguing in an easy style.
Then, looking, I saw Love come silently,
habited in black raiment, smooth and new,
    having a black hat set upon his hair;
and certainly the tears he shed were true.
    So that I asked, "What ails you, trifler?"
Answering he said: "A grief to be gone through;
    for our own lady's dying, brother dear."

Dante Alighieri
Canzone: He beseeches Death for the life of Beatrice

Death, since I find not one with whom to grieve,
    nor whom this grief of mine may move to tears,
        whereso I be or whitherso I turn:
since it is you who in my soul will leave
    no single joy, but chill it with just fears
        and make it in fruitless hopes to burn:
        since you, Death, and you only, can decern
wealth to my life, or want, at your free choice—
it is to you that I lift up my voice,
    bowing my face that's like a face just dead.
I come to you, as to one pitying,
in grief for that sweet rest which nought can bring
    again, if you but once be entered
into her life whom my heart cherishes
even as the only portal of its peace.

Death, how most sweet the peace is that your grace
    can grant to me, and that I pray you for,
        you easily may know by a sure sign,
if in my eyes you look a little space
    and read in them the hidden dread they store—
        if upon all you look which proves me yours.
        Since the fear only makes me to pine
after this sort—what will my anguish be
when her eyes close, of dreadful verity,
    in whose light is the light of my own eyes?
But now I know that you would have my life
as hers, and joys you in my fruitless strife.
    Yet I do think this which I feel implies
that soon, when I would die to flee from pain,
I shall find none by whom I may be slain.

Death, if indeed you smite this gentle one
    whose outward worth but tells the intellect
        how wondrous is the miracle within—
you bid Virtue rise up and begone,
    you do away with Mercy's best effect,
        you spoil the mansion of God's sojourning.
        Yea, unto nought her beauty you do bring

which is above all other beauties, even
in so much as befits one whom Heaven
	sent upon earth in token of its own.
You do break through the perfect trust which has
been alway her companion in Love's path:
	the light once darkened which was hers alone,
Love needs must say to them he rules over,
"I have lost the noble banner that I bore."

Death, have some pity then for all the ill
	which cannot chose but happen if she die,
		and which will be the sorest ever known.
Slacken the string, if so it be your will,
	that the sharp arrow leave it not—thereby
		sparing her life, which if it flies is flown.
		O Death, for God's sake, be some pity shown!
Restrain within yourself, even at its height,
the cruel wrath which moves you to smite
	her in whom God has set so much of grace.
Show now some ruth if 'tis a thing you have!
I seem to see Heaven's gate, that is shut fast,
	open, and angels filling all the space
about me—come to fetch her soul whose laud
is sung by saints and angels before God.

Song, you must surely see how fine a thread
	this is that my last hope is holden by,
		and what I should be brought to without her.
Therefore for your plain speech and lowlihead
	make you no pause; but go immediately
		(knowing yourself for my heart's minister),
		and with that very meek and piteous air
you have, stand up before the face of Death,
to wrench away the bar that prisons
	and win unto the place of the good fruit.
And if indeed you shake by your soft voice
Death's mortal purpose—haste you and rejoice
	our lady with the issue of your suit.
So yet awhile our earthly nights and days
shall keep the blessed spirit that I praise.

CINO DA PISTOIA

Sonnet to Dante Alighieri: He conceives of some compensation in death

Dante, whenever this thing happens—
    that love's desire is quite bereft of hope
    (seeking in vain at ladies' eyes some scope
of joy, through what the heart forever says)—
I ask you, can amends be made by death?
    Is such sad pass the last extremity—
    Or may the soul that never feared to die
then in another body draw new breath?
Lo! thus it is through her who governs all
    below—that I, who entered at her door,
        now at her dreadful window must fare forth.
Yea, and I think through her it does befall
    that even ere yet the road is travelled over
        my bones are weary and life is nothing worth.

Giovanni Boccaccio

Sonnet: To Dante in Paradise, after Fiammetta's death

Dante, if you within the sphere of Love,
    as I believe, remain contemplating
    beautiful Beatrice, whom you did sing
erewhile, and so were drawn to her above—
unless from false life true life you remove
    so far that Love's forgotten, let me bring
    one prayer before you: for an easy thing
this were, to you whom I do ask it of.
I know that where all joy does most abound
    in the third Heaven, my own Fiammetta sees
        the grief which I have borne since she is dead.
O pray her (if my image be not drowned
    in Lethe) that her prayers may never cease
        until I reach her and am comforted.

Cino da Pistoia

Canzone to Dante Alighieri: On the death of Beatrice Portinari

Albeit my prayers have not so long delayed,
    but craved for you, ere this, that Pity and Love
    which only bring our heavy life some rest;
yet is not now the time so much overstayed
    but that these words of mine which towards you move
        must find you still with spirit dispossessed,
        and say to you: "In Heaven she now is blessed,
even as the blessed name men called her by";
        while you do ever cry,
"Alas! the blessing of my eyes is flown!"
        Behold, these words set down
    are needed still, for still you sorrow.
Then hearken; I would yield advisedly
some comfort: Stay these sighs; give ear to me.

Guido Cavalcanti

Sonnet to Dante Alighieri: He rebukes Dante for his way of life, after the death of Beatrice

I come to you by daytime constantly,
> but in your thoughts too much of baseness find:
> greatly it grieves me for your gentle mind,

and for your many virtues gone from you.
It was your wont to shun much company,
> unto all sorry concourse ill inclined:
> and still your speech of me, heartfelt and kind,

had made me treasure up your poetry.
But now I dare not, for your abject life,
> make manifest that I approve your rhymes;
>> nor come I in such sort that you may know.

Ah! pray you read this sonnet many times:
so shall that evil one who bred this strife
> be thrust from your dishonored soul and go.

Dante Alighieri

Sonnet: To the lady Pietra degli Scrovigni

My curse be on the day when first I saw
> the brightness in those treacherous eyes of yours—

the hour when from my heart you came to draw
> my soul away, that both might fail and pine:
> my curse be on the skill that smoothed each line

of my vain songs—the music and just law
> of art, by which it was my dear design

that the whole world should yield you love and awe.
Yea, let me curse my own obduracy,
> which firmly holds what does itself confound—
>> to wit, your fair perverted face of scorn:
>> for whose sake Love is oftentimes forsworn

so that men mock at him: but most at me
> who would hold fortune's wheel and turn it round.

Dante Alighieri

Sestina: Of the lady Pietra degli Scrovigni

To the dim light and the large circle of shade
I have clomb, and to the whitening of the hills,
there where we see no color in the grass.
Natheless my longing loses not its green,
it has so taken root in the hard stone
which talks and hears as though it were a lady.

Utterly frozen is this youthful lady,
even as the snow that lies within the shade;
for she is no more moved than is the stone
by the sweet season which makes warm the hills
and alters them afresh from white to green,
covering their sides again with flowers and grass.

On Death

GUIDO GUINICELLI

Sonnet: *Of human presumption*

Among my thoughts I count it wonderful,
   how foolish in man should be so rife
   that masterly he takes the world to wife
as though no end were set unto his rule:
in labor alway that his ease be full,
   as though there never were another life;
   till Death throws all his order into strife,
and round his head his purposes does pull.
And evermore one sees the other die,
   and sees how all conditions turn to change,
      yet in no wise may the blind wretch be healed.
   I therefore say, that sin can even estrange
man's very sight, and his heart satisfy
      to live as lives a sheep upon the field.

Cecco Angiolieri

Sonnet: He argues his case with Death

Gramercy, Death, as you've my love to win,
    just be impartial in your next assault;
    and that you may not find yourself in fault,
whatever you do, be quick now and begin.
As oft may I be pounded flat and thin
    as in Grosseto there are grains of salt,
    if not to kill us both you be not called—
both me and him who sticks so in his skin.
Or better still, look here; for if I'm slain
    alone—his wealth, it's true, I'll never have,
yet death is life to one who lives in pain:
    but if you only kill Saldagno's knave,
I'm left in Siena (don't you see your gain?)
    like a rich man who's made a galley-slave.

Guido Cavalcanti

Ballata: He perceives that his highest love is gone from him

Through this my strong and new misaventure,
    all now is lost to me
which most was sweet in Love's supremacy.

So much of life is dead in its control,
    that she, my pleasant lady of all grace,
is gone out of the devastated soul:
    I see her not, nor do I know her place;
    nor even enough of virtue with me stays
        to understand, ah me!
the flower of her exceeding purity.

Because there comes—to kill that gentle thought
    with saying that I shall not see her more—
this constant pain wherewith I am distraught,
    which is a burning torment very sore,
    wherein I know not whom I should implore.
        Thrice thanked the Master be
who turns the grinding wheel of misery!

Full of great anguish in a place of fear
    the spirit of my heart lies sorrowing,
through Fortune's bitter craft. She lured it here,
    and gave it over to Death, and barbed the sting;
she wrought that hope which was a treacherous thing;
        in Time, which dies from me,
she made me lose my hour of ecstasy.

For you, perturbed and fearful words of mine,
    whither yourselves may please, even thither go;
but always burdened with shame's troublous sign,
    and on my lady's name still calling low.
    For me, I must abide in such deep woe
        that all who look shall see
Death's shadow on my face assuredly.

DANTE ALIGHIERI

Sonnet to certain ladies: When Beatrice was lamenting her father's death

Whence come you, all of you so sorrowful?
    An it may please you, speak for courtesy.
    I fear for my dear lady's sake, lest she
have made you to return thus filled with dule.
O gentle ladies, be not hard to school
    in gentleness, but to some pause agree,
    and something of my lady say to me,
for with a little my desire is full.
Howbeit it be a heavy thing to hear:
    for Love now utterly has thrust me forth,
with hand forever lifted, striking fear.
    See if I be not worn unto the earth;
yea, and my spirit must fail from me here,
    if, when you speak, your words are of no worth.

Dante Alighieri

Sonnet to the same ladies: With their answer

You ladies, walking past me piteous-eyed,
    who is the lady that lies prostrate here?
    Can this be even she my heart holds dear?
Nay, if it be so, speak, and nothing hide.
Her very aspect seems itelf beside,
    and all her features of such altered cheer
    that to my thinking they do not appear
hers who makes other seem beatified.

"If you forget to know our lady thus,
    whom grief overcomes, we wonder in no wise,
for also the same thing befalls us.
    Yet if you watch the movement of her eyes,
of her you shall be straightway conscious.
    O weep no more; you are all wan with sighs."

Onesto di Boncima

Sonnet: Of the Last Judgment

Upon that cruel season when our Lord
    shall come to judge the world eternally;
when to no one shall anything afford
    peace in the heart, how pure soever it be;
when Heaven shall break asunder at his word,
    with a great trembling of the earth and sea;
when even the just shall fear the dreadful sword—
    the wicked crying, "Where shall I cover me?"—
when no one angel in his presence stands
    that shall not be affrighted of that wrath,
        except the Virgin Lady, she our guide—
how shall I then escape, whom sin commands?
    Out and alas on me! There is no path,
        if in her prayers I be not justified.

Cino da Pistoia

Sonnet: *Of the grave of Selvaggia, on the Monte della Sambuca*

I was upon the high and blessed mound,
    and kissed, long worshipping, the stones and grass,
    there on the hard stones prostrate, where, alas!
that pure one laid her forehead in the ground.
Then were the springs of gladness sealed and bound,
    the day that unto Death's most bitter pass
    my sick heart's lady turned her feet, who was
already in her gracious life renowned.
So in that place I spoke to Love, and cried:
    "O sweet my god, I am one whom Death may claim
    hence to be his; for lo! my heart lies here."
    Anon, because my Master lent no ear,
    departing, still I called Selvaggia's name.
So with my moan I left the mountainside.

Cino da Pistoia

Canzone: *His lament for Selvaggia*

Ay me, alas! the beautiful bright hair
    that shed reflected gold
        over the green growths on either side the way:
Ay me! the lovely look, open and fair,
    which my heart's core does hold
        with all else of that best-remembered day;
        Ay me! the face made gay
with joy that Love confers;
Ay me! that smile of hers
    where whiteness as of snow was visible
among the roses at all seasons red!
        Ay me! and was this well,
O Death, to let me live when she is dead?

Ay me! the calm, erect, dignified walk;
    Ay me! the sweet salute—
        the thoughtful mind—the wit discreetly worn;

Ay me! the clearness of her noble talk,
    which made the good take root
        in me, and for the evil woke my scorn;
    Ay me! the longing born
of so much loveliness—
the hope, whose eager stress
    made other hopes fall back to let it pass,
even till my load of love grew light thereby!
    These you have broken, as glass,
O Death, who makes me, alive, to die!

Ay me! Lady, the lady of all worth—
    saint, for whose single shrine
        all other shrines I left, even as Love willed—
Ay me! what precious stone in the whole earth,
    for that pure fame of yours
        worthy the marble statue's base to yield?
    Ay me! fair vase fulfilled
with more than this world's good—
by cruel chance and rude
    cast out upon the steep path of the mountains
where Death has shut you in between hard stones!
    Ay me! two languid fountains
of weeping are these eyes, which joy disowns.

Ay me, sharp Death! till what I ask is done
    and my whole life is ended utterly—
answer—must I weep on
    even thus, and never cease to moan Ay me?

Guido Cavalcanti

Canzone: A dispute with Death

"O sluggish, hard, ingrate, what do you?
    Poor sinner, folded round with heavy sin,
        whose life to find out joy alone is bent.
I call you, and you fall to deafness now;
    and, deeming that my path whereby to win
        your seat is lost, there sit you down content,
        and hold me to your will subservient.
But I into your heart have crept disguised:
    among your senses and your sins I went,
by roads you did not guess, unrecognized.
Tears will not now suffice to bid me go,
nor countenance abased, nor words of woe."

Now, when I heard the sudden dreadful voice
    wake thus within to cruel utterance,
        whereby the very heart of hearts did fail,
my spirit might not any more rejoice,
    but fell from its courageous pride at once,
        and turned to fly, where flight may not avail.
        Then slowly 'gan some strength to re-inhale
the trembling life which heard that whisper speak,
    and had conceived the sense with sore travail,
till in the mouth it murmured, very weak,
saying: "Youth, wealth, and beauty, these have I:
O Death! remit your claim—I would not die."

Small sign of pity in that aspect dwells
    which then had scattered all my life abroad
        till there was comfort with no single sense;
and yet almost in piteous syllables,
    when I had ceased to speak, this answer flowed:
        "Behold what path is spread before you hence,
        your life has all but a day's permanence.
And is it for the sake of youth there seems
    in loss of human years such sore offense?
Nay, look unto the end of youthful dreams.
What present glory does your hope possess,
that shall not yield ashes and bitterness?"

But, when I looked on Death made visible,
    from my heart's sojourn brought before my eyes,
        and holding in her hand my grievous sin,
I seemed to see my countenance, that fell,
    shake like a shadow; my heart uttered cries,
        and my soul wept the curse that lay therein.
        Then Death: "Thus much your urgent prayer shall win—
I grant you the brief interval of youth
    at natural pity's strong soliciting."
And I (because I knew that moment's ruth
but left my life to groan for a frail space)
fell in the dust upon my weeping face.

So, when she saw me thus abashed and dumb,
    in loftier words she weighed her argument,
        that new and strange it was to hear her speak;
saying: "The path your fears withhold you from
is your best path. To folly be not shent,
        nor shrink from me because your flesh is weak.
        You see how man is sore confused, and eke
how ruinous Chance makes havoc of his life,
        and grief is in the joys that he does seek;
nor ever pauses the perpetual strife
'twixt fear and rage; until beneath the sun
his perfect anguish be fulfilled and done."

"O Death! you are so dark and difficult,
    that never human creature might attain
        by his own will to pierce your secret sense,
because, foreshadowing your dread result,
he may not put his trust in heart or brain,
        nor power avails him, nor intelligence.
        Behold how cruelly you take hence
these forms so beautiful and dignified,
        and chain them in your shadow chill and dense,
and force them in narrow graves to hide;
with pitiless hate subduing still to you
the strength of man and woman's delicacy."

"Not for your fear the less I come at last,
    for this your tremor, for your painful sweat.
        Take therefore thought to leave (for lo! I call)
kinsfolk and comrades, all you did hold fast—
    your father and your mother—to forget
        all these your brethren, sisters, children, all.
        Cast sight and hearing from you; let hope fall;
leave every sense and your whole intellect,
    these things wherein your life made festival:
for I have wrought you to such strange effect
that you have no more power to dwell with these
    as living man. Let pass your soul in peace."

Yea, Lord. O you, the Builder of the spheres,
    who, making me, did shape me, of your grace,
        in your own image and high counterpart;
do you subdue my spirit, long perverse,
    to weep within your will a certain space,
        ere yet your thunder come to rive my heart.
        Set in my hand some sign of what you are,
Lord God, and suffer me to seek out Christ—
    weeping, to seek Him in your ways apart;
until my sorrow have at length sufficed
in some accepted instant to atone
for sins of thought, for stubborn evil done.

Dishevelled, and in tears, go, song of mine,
    to break the hardness of the heart of man:
        say how his life began
from dust, and in that dust does sink supine:
    yet, say, the unerring spirit of grief shall guide
        his soul, being purified,
to seek its Maker at the heavenly shrine.

On Poverty

GIOTTO DI BONDONE
Canzone: Of the doctrine of voluntary poverty

Many there are, praisers of Poverty;
the which as man's best state is registered
    when by free choice preferred,
with strict observance having nothing here.
For this they find certain authority
wrought of an over-nice interpreting.
    Now as concerns such thing,
a hard extreme it does to me appear,
    which to commend I fear,
for seldom are extremes without some vice.
    Let every edifice,
of work or word, secure foundation find;
    against the potent wind,
and all things perilous, so well prepared
that it need no correction afterward.

Of poverty which is against the will,
it never can be doubted that therein
    lies broad the way to sin.
For oftentimes it makes the judge unjust;
in dames and damsels does their honor kill;
and begets violence and villanies,
    and theft and wicked lies,
and casts a good man from his fellows' trust.
    And for a little dust
of gold that lacks, wit seems a lacking too.
    If once the coat give view
of the real back, farewell all dignity.
    Each therefore strives that he
should by no means admit her to his sight,
who, only thought on, makes his face turn white.

Of poverty which seems by choice elect,
I may pronounce from plain experience—
      not of my own pretense—
that 'tis observed or unobserved at will.

Nor its observance asks our full respect:
for no discernment, nor integrity,
      nor lore of life, nor plea
of virtue, can her cold regard instill.
      I call it shame and ill
to name as virtue that which stifles good.
      I call it grossly rude,
on a thing bestial to make consequent
      virtue's inspired advent
to understanding hearts acceptable:
for the most wise most love with her to dwell.

Here may you find some issue of demur:
for lo! our Lord commends poverty.
      Nay, what His meaning be
search well: His words are wonderfully deep,
oft doubly sensed, asking interpreter.
The state for each most saving, is His will
      for each. Your eyes unseal,
and look within, the inmost truth to reap;
      behold what concord keep
His holy words with His most holy life.
      In Him the power was rife
which to all things apportions time and place.
      On earth He chose such case;
and why? 'Twas His to point a higher life.

But here, on earth, our senses show us still
how they who preach this thing are least at peace,
      and evermore increase
much thought how from this thing they should escape.
For if one such a lofty station fill,
he shall assert his strength like a wild wolf,
      or daily mask himself
afresh, until his will be brought to shape;
      ay, and so wear the cape
that direst wolf shall seem like sweetest lamb
      beneath the constant sham.

Hence, by their art, this doctrine plagues the world:
    and hence, till they be hurled
from where they sit in high hypocrisy,
no corner of the world seems safe to me.
Go, Song, to some sworn owls that we have known,
and on their folly bring them to reflect:
    but if they be stiff-necked,
belabor them until their heads are down.

GUIDO CAVALCANTI

Canzone: A song against poverty

O poverty, by you the soul is wrapped
    with hate, with envy, dolefulness, and doubt.
        Even so be you cast out,
    and even so he that speaks you otherwise.
I name you now, because my mood is apt
to curse you, bride of every lost estate,
        through whom are desolate
    on earth all honorable things and wise.
    Within your power each blessed condition dies:
By you, men's minds with sore mistrust are made
        fantastic and afraid—
You, hated worse than Death, by just accord,
and with the loathing of all hearts abhorred.
Yea, rightly are you hated worse than Death,
    for he at length is longed for in the breast.
        But not with you, wild beast,
    was ever aught found beautiful or good.
For life is all that man can lose by death,
not fame and the fair summits of applause;
        his glory shall not pause,
    but live in men's perpetual gratitude.
    While he who on your naked sill has stood,
though of great heart and worthy everso,
        he shall be counted low.
Then let the man you trouble never hope
to spread his wings in any lofty scope.

Hereby my mind is laden with a fear,
    and I will take some thought to shelter me.
        For this I plainly see—
    through you, to fraud the honest man is led;
to tyranny the just lord turns here,
and the magnanimous soul to avarice.
        Of every bitter vice
    you, to my thinking, are the fount and head;
    from you no light in any wise is shed,
who brings to the paths of dusky hell.
        I therefore see full well,
that death, the dungeon, sickness, and old age,
weighed against you, are blessed heritage.

And what though many a goodly hypocrite,
    lifting to you his veritably prayer,
        call God to witness there
    how this your burden moved not Him to wrath.
Why, who may call (of them that muse aright)
him poor, who of the whole can say, 'Tis mine?
        Methinks I well divine
    that want, to such, should seem an easy path.
    God, who made all things, all things had and has;
nor any tongue may say that He was poor,
        what while He did endure
for man's best succor among men to dwell:
since to have all, with Him, was possible.

Song, you shall wend upon your journey now:
    and, if you meet with folk who rail at you,
        saying that poverty
is not even sharper than your words allow—
unto such brawlers briefly answer you,
to tell them they are hypocrites; and then
        say mildly, once again,
that I, who am nearly in a beggar's case,
might not presume to sing my proper praise.

CECCO ANGIOLIERI

Sonnet: He is past all help

For a thing done, repentance is no good,
    nor to say after, Thus would I have done:
in life, what's left behind is vainly rued;
    so let a man get used his heart to shun;
for on his legs he hardly may be stood
    again, if once his fall be well begun.
But to show wisdom's what I never could;
    so where I itch I scratch now, and all's one.
I'm down, and cannot rise in any way;
    for not a creature of my nearest kin
        would hold me out a hand that I could reach.
I pray you do not mock at what I say;
    for so my love's good grace may I not win
        if ever sonnet held so true a speech!

Guido Cavalcanti

Canzone: A Song of Fortune

Lo! I am she who makes the wheel to turn;
    Lo! I am she who gives and takes away;
        blamed idly, day by day,
    in all my acts by you, you mankind.
for whoso smites his visage and does mourn,
    what time he renders back my gifts to me,
        learns then that I decree
    no state which my own arrows may not find.
    Who clomb must fall—this bear you well in mind,
nor say, because he fell, I did him wrong.
        Yet mine is a vain song;
for truly you may find out wisdom when
King Arthur's resting-place is found of men.
You make great marvel and astonishment
    what time you see the sluggard lifted up
        and the just one to drop,
    and you complain on God and on my sway.
O mankind, you sin in your complaint:
    for He, that Lord who made the world to live,
        lets me not take or give
    by my own act, but as he wills I may.
    Yet is the mind of man so castaway,
that it discerns not the supreme behest.
        Alas! you wretchedest,
and chide you at God also? Shall not He
judge between good and evil righteously?

Ah! had you knowledge how God evermore,
    with agonies of soul and grievous heats,
        as on an anvil beats
    on them that in this earth hold high estate—
you would choose little rather than much store,
    and solitude than spacious palaces;
        such is the sore disease
    of anguish that on all their days does wait.
    Behold if they be not unfortunate,
when oft the father dares not trust the son!
        O wealth, with you is won

a worm to gnaw forever on his soul
whose abject life is laid in your control!

If also you take note what piteous death
    they oft-times make, whose hoards were manifold,
        who cities had and gold
    and multitudes of men beneath their hand;
then he among you that most angers
    shall bless me, saying, "Lo! I worship you
        that I was not as he
    whose death is thus accurst throughout the land."
But now your living souls are held in band
of avarice, shutting you from the true light
        which shows how sad and slight
are this world's treasured riches and array
that still change hands a hundred times a day.

For me—could envy enter in my sphere,
    which of all human taint is clean and quit—
        I well might harbor it
    when I behold the peasant at his toil.
Guiding his team, untroubled, free from fear,
    he leaves his perfect furrow as he goes,
        and gives his field repose
    from thorns and tares and weeds that vex the soil:
thereto he labors, and without turmoil
entrusts his work to God, content if so
        such guerdon from it grow
that in that year his family shall live:
nor care nor thought to other things will give.

But now you may no more have speech of me,
    for this my office craves continual use:
        you therefore deeply muse
    upon those things which you have heard the while:
yea, and even yet remember heedfully
    how this my wheel a motion has so fleet,
        that in an eyelid's beat
    him whom it raised it makes low and vile.
    None was, nor is, nor shall be of such guile,
who could, or can, or shall, I say, at length
        prevail against my strength.

But still those men that are my questioners
in bitter torment own their hearts perverse.

Song, that was made to carry high intent
    dissembled in the garb of humbleness—
        with fair and open face
to Master Thomas let your course be bent.
Say that a great thing scarcely may be pent
    in little room: yet always pray that he
        commend us, you and me,
to them that are more apt in lofty speech:
for truly one must learn ere he can teach.

CECCO ANGIOLIERI

Sonnet: *Of why he would be a scullion*

I am so out of love through poverty
    that if I see my mistress in the street
    I can hardly can be certain whom I meet,
and of her name do scarce remember me.
Also my courage it has made to be
    so cold, that if I suffered some foul cheat,
    even from the meanest wretch that one could beat,
save for the sin I think he should go free.
Ay, and it plays me a still nastier trick;
    for, meeting some who erewhile with me took
        delight, I seem to them a roaring fire.
So here's a truth whereat I need not stick—
    that if one could turn scullion to a cook,
        it were a thing to which one might aspire.

Cecco Angiolieri

Sonnet: *Of why he is unhanged*

Whoever without money is in love
    had better build a gallows and go hang;
    he dies not once, but oftener feels the pang
than he who was cast down from Heaven above.
And certes, for my sins it's plain enough,
    if Love's alive on earth, that he's myself,
    who would not be so cursed with want of pelf
if others paid my proper dues thereof.
They why am I not hanged by my own hands?
    I answer: for this empty narrow chink
        of hope—that I've a father old and rich,
and that if once he dies I'll get his lands;
    and die he must, when the sea's dry, I think
Meanwhile God keeps him whole and me in the ditch.

Controversies and Politics

CINO DA PISTOIA

Sonnet to Guido Cavalcanti: *He owes nothing to Guido as a poet*

What rhymes are yours which I have taken from you,
    you Guido, that you ever said I thieve?
    'Tis true, fine fancies gladly I receive,
but when was aught found beautiful in you?
Nay, I have searched my pages diligently,
    and tell the truth, and lie not, by your leave.
    From whose rich store my web of songs I weave
Love knows well, well knowing them and me.
No artist I—all men may gather it;
    nor do I work in ignorance of pride,
        (though the world reach alone the coarser sense)
but am a certain man of humble wit
    who journeys with his sorrow at his side,
        for a heart's sake, alas! that is gone hence.

Giovanni Boccaccio

Sonnet: To one who had censured his public exposition of Dante

If Dante mourns, there wheresoever he be,
   that such high fancies of a soul so proud
   should be laid open to the vulgar crowd
(as, touching my Discourse, I'm told by you)
this were my grievous pain; and certainly
   my proper blame should not be disavowed;
   though hereof somewhat, I declare aloud
were due to others, not alone to me.
False hopes, true poverty, and therewithal
   the blinded judgment of a host of friends,
     and their entreaties, made that I did thus.
But of all this there is no gain at all
   unto the thankless souls with whose base ends
     nothing agrees that's great or generous.

Guido Cavalcanti

Ballata: In exile at Sarzana

Because I think not ever to return,
   Ballad, to Tuscany—
   go therefore you for me
     straight to my lady's face,
     who, of her noble grace,
   shall show you courtesy.

You seek her in change of many sighs,
   full of much grief and of exceeding fear.
But have good heed you come not to the eyes
   of such as are sworn foes to gentle cheer:
   for, certes, if this thing should chance—from her
     You then could only look
     for scorn, and such rebuke
     as needs must bring me pain—
     yea, after death again
     tears and fresh agony.

Surely you know, Ballad, how that Death
    assails me, till my life is almost sped:
you know how my heart still travails
    through the sore pangs which in my soul are bred—
    my body being now so nearly dead,
        it cannot suffer more.
        Then, going, I implore
        that this my soul you take
        (nay, do so for my sake)
        when my heart sets it free.

Ah! Ballad, unto your dear offices
    I do commend my soul, thus trembling;
that you may lead it, for pure piteousness,
    even to that lady's presence whom I sing.
    Ah! Ballad, say you to her, sorrowing,
        whereso you meet her then—
        "This your poor handmaiden
        is come, nor will be gone,
        being parted now from one
        who served Love painfully."

You also, you bewildered voice and weak,
    that go forth in tears from my grieved heart,
shall, with my soul and with this ballad, speak
    of my dead mind, when you do hence depart,
    unto that lady (piteous as you are!)
        who is so calm and bright,
        it shall be deep delight
        to feel her presence there.
        And you, Soul, worship her
        still in her purity.

CECCO ANGIOLIERI

Sonnet to Dante Alighieri: He writes to Dante, then in exile at Verona, defying him as no better than himself

Dante Alighieri, if I jest and lie,
>you in such lists might run a tilt with me:
>I get my dinner, you your supper, free;
and if I bite the fat, you suck the fry;
I shear the cloth and you the teazel ply;
>if I've a strut, who's prouder than you are?
If I'm foul-mouthed, you're not particular;
and you're turned Lombard, even if Roman I.
So that, 'fore Heaven! if either of us flings
>much dirt at the other, he must be a fool:
for lack of luck and wit we do these things.
>Yet if you want more lessons at my school,
just say so, and you'll find the next touch stings—
>for, Dante, I'm the goad and you're the bull.

DANTE ALIGHIERI

Sonnet to Forese Donati: He taunts Forese, by the nickname of Bicci

O Bicci, pretty son of who knows whom
>unless your mother Lady Tessa tell—
>your gullet is already crammed too well,
yet others' food you needs must now consume.
Lo! he that wears a purse makes ample room
>when you go by in any public place,
>saying, "This fellow with the branded face
is thief apparent from his mother's womb."
And I know one who's fain to keep his bed
>lest you should filch it, at whose birth he stood
>>like Joseph when the world its Christmas saw.
Of Bicci and his brothers it is said
>that with the heat of misbegotten blood
>>among their wives they are nice brothers-in-law.

Forese Donati

Sonnet to Dante Alighieri: He taunts Dante ironically for not avenging his father, Geri Alighieri

Right well I know you are Alighieri's son;
    nay, that revenge alone might warrant it,
    which you did take, so clever and complete,
for your great-uncle who awhile agone
paid scores in full. Why, if you had hewn one
    in bits for it, 'twere early still for peace!
    But then your head's so heaped with things like these
that they would weigh two sumpter-horses down.
You have taught us a fair fashion, sooth to say—
    that whoso lays a stick well to your back,
        your comrade and your brother he shall be.
As for their names who've shown you this good play,
    I'll tell them you, so you will tell me back
        all of your fears, that I may stand by you.

Dante Alighieri

Sonnet to Forese Donati: He taunts him concerning his wife

To hear the unlucky wife of Bicci cough,
    (Bicci—Forese as he's called, you know)
you'd fancy she had wintered, sure enough,
    where icebergs rear themselves in constant snow;
    and Lord! if in mid-August it is so,
how in the frozen months must she come off?
    To wear her socks abed avails not—no,
nor quilting from Cortona, warm and tough.
Her cough, her cold, and all her other ills,
    do not afflict her through the rheum of age,
        but through some want within her nest, poor spouse!
This grief, with other griefs, her mother feels,
    why says, "Without much trouble, I'll engage
        she might have married in Count Guido's house!"

Forese Donati

Sonnet to Dante Alighieri: He taunts him concerning the unavenged spirit of Geri Alighieri

The other night I had a dreadful cough
   because I'd got no bedclothes over me;
and so, when the day broke, I hurried off
   to seek some gain whatever it might be.
And such luck as I had I tell you of.
   For lo! no jewels hidden in a tree
I find, nor buried gold, nor suchlike stuff,
   but Alighieri among the graves I see,
bound by some spell, I know not at whose 'hest—
   at Solomon's, or what sage's who shall say?
Therefore I crossed myself towards the east;
   and he cried out: "For Dante's love I pray
you loose me!" But I knew not in the least
   how this were done, so turned and went my way.

Guido Cavalcanti

Sonnet to Pope Boniface VIII: After the Pope's Interdict, when the great houses were leaving Florence

Nero, thus much for tidings in your ear.
   They of the Buondelmonti quake with dread,
   nor by all Florence may be comforted,
noting in you the lion's ravenous cheer;
who more than any dragon give them fear,
   in ancient evil stubbornly arrayed;
   neither by bridge nor bulwark to be stayed,
but only by King Pharaoh's sepulcher.
Oh, in what monstrous sin do you engage—
   all these which are of loftiest blood to drive
     away, that none dare pause but all take wing!
Yet sooth it is, you might redeem the pledge
   even yet, and save your naked soul alive,
     were you but patient in the bargaining.

GUIDO ORLANDI

Sonnet: Against the "White" Ghibellines

Now of the hue of ashes are the Whites;
    and they go following now after the kind
    of creatures we call crabs, which, as some find,
will only seek their natural food o' nights.
All day they hide; their flesh has such sore frights
    lest Death be come for them on every wind,
    lest now the Lion's wrath be so inclined
that they may never set their sin to rights.
Guelf were they once, and now are Ghibelline:
    nothing but rebels henceforth be they named—
    state-foes, as are the Uberti, every one.
Behold, against the Whites all men must sign
    some judgment whence no pardon can be claimed
        excepting they were offered to Saint John.

SIMONE DALL' ANTELLA

Prolonged Sonnet: In the last days of Emperor Henry VII

Along the road all shapes must travel by,
    how swiftly, to my thinking, now does fare
    the wanderer who built his watchtower there
where wind is torn with wind continually!
Lo! from the world and its dull pain to fly,
    unto such pinnacle did he repair,
    and of her presence was not made aware,
whose face, that looks like Peace, is Death's own lie.
Alas, Ambition, you his enemy,
    who lures the poor wanderer on his way,
but never brings him where his rest may be—
    O leave him now, for he is gone astray
himself out of his very self through you,
    till now the broken stems his feet betray,
and, caught with boughs before and boughs behind,
deep in your tangled wood he sinks entwined.

Index of First Lines

A certain youthful lady in Toulouse	
Guido Cavalcanti	30
A day agone, as I rode sullenly	
Dante Alighieri	77
A gentle thought there is will often start	
Dante Alighieri	128
A lady in whom love is manifest—	
Guido Cavalcanti	41
Albeit my prayers have not so long delayed	
Cino da Pistoia	140
All my thoughts always speak to me of love	
Dante Alighieri	84
All you that pass along Love's trodden way	
Dante Alighieri	73
Along the road all shapes must travel by	
Simone dall' Antella	167
Among my thoughts I count it wonderful	
Guido Guinicelli	143
As you were loathe to see, before your feet	
Guido Cavalcanti	26
At whiles (yea oftentimes) I muse over	
Dante Alighieri	90
A very pitiful lady, very young	
Dante Alighieri	103
Ay me, alas! the beautiful bright hair	
Cino da Pistoia	147
Ballad, since Love himself has fashioned you	
Lappo Gianni	22

Beauty in women; the high will's decree Guido Cavalcanti	28
Because I think not ever to return Guido Cavalcanti	162
Because my eyes can never have their fill Dante Alighieri	41
Being in thought of love, I chanced to see Guido Cavalcanti	31
Beyond the sphere which spreads to widest space Dante Alighieri	133
Can you indeed be he that still would sing Dante Alighieri	100
Dante, a sigh that rose from the heart's core Guido Cavalcanti	20
Dante Alighieri, if I jest and lie Cecco Angiolieri	164
Dante Alighieri in Becchina's praise Cecco Angiolieri	26
Dante, if you within the sphere of Love Giovanni Boccaccio	140
Dante, since I from my own native place Cino da Pistoia	56
Dante, whenever this thing happens— Cino da Pistoia	139
Death, always cruel, Pity's foe in chief Dante Alighieri	75
Death, since I find not one with whom to grieve Dante Alighieri	137
Even as the others mock, you mock me Dante Alighieri	87
Flowers have you in yourself, and foliage Guido Cavalcanti	29

For a thing done, repentance is no good Cecco Angiolieri	156
For certain he has seen all perfectness Dante Alighieri	112
Friend, well I know you know well to bear Guido Orlandi	36
Gramercy, Death, as you've my love to win Cecco Angiolieri	144
Guido, an image of my lady dwells Guido Cavalcanti	62
Guido, I wish that Lappo, you, and I Dante Alighieri	20
Guido, that Gianni who, a day agone Gianni Alfani	33
He that has grown to wisdom hurries not Guido Guinicelli	56
I am all bent to glean the golden ore Cino da Pistoia	46
I am enamored, and yet not so much Cecco Angiolieri	54
I am so out of love through poverty Cecco Angiolieri	159
I come to you by daytime constantly Guido Cavalcanti	141
If, as you say, your love torments you Terino da Castel Fiorentino	43
If Dante mourns, there wheresoever he be Giovanni Boccaccio	162
I felt a spirit of love begin to stir Dante Alighieri	107
If I'd a sack of florins, and all new Cecco Angiolieri	48

If I entreat this lady that all grace Guido Cavalcanti	38
If I were fire, I'd burn the world away Cecco Angiolieri	62
If I were still that man, worthy to love Guido Cavalcanti	21
If you had offered, friend, to blessed Mary Guido Orlandi	63
I hold him, verily, of mean emprise Guido Guinicelli	58
I'm caught, like any thrush the nets surprise Cecco Angiolieri	49
I'm full of everything I do not want Cecco Angiolieri	27
I pray you, Dante, should you meet with Love Guido Cavalcanti	21
I thought to be forever separate Dante Alighieri	55
I was upon the high and blessed mound Cino da Pistoia	147
I would like better in the grace to be Cecco Angiolieri	25
Just look, Manetto, at that wry-mouthed minx Guido Cavalcanti	38
Ladies that have intelligence in love Dante Alighieri	93
Last All Saints' holy-day, even now gone by Dante Alighieri	45
Let no one predicate Guido Guinicelli	
Let not the inhabitants of Hell despair Cecco Angiolieri	50

Lo! I am she who makes the wheel to turn Guido Cavalcanti	157
Love and the gentle heart are one same thing Dante Alighieri	96
Love and the lady Lagia, Guido and I Guido Cavalcanti	23
Love has so long possessed me for his own Dante Alighieri	113
Love, I demand to have my lady in fee Lappo Gianni	19
Love's pallor and the semblance of deep ruth Dante Alighieri	125
Many there are, praisers of Poverty; Giotto di Bondone	152
Master Brunetto, this my little maid Dante Alighieri	66
My curse be on the day when first I saw Dante Alighieri	141
My eyes beheld the blessed pity spring Dante Alighieri	124
My heart's so heavy with a hundred things Cecco Angiolieri	25
My lady carries love within her eyes Dante Alighieri	97
My lady looks so gentle and so pure Dante Alighieri	111
Nero, thus much for tidings in your ear. Guido Cavalcanti	166
No man may mount upon a golden stair Dino Compagni	37
Now of the hue of ashes are the Whites Guido Orlandi	167

O Bicci, pretty son of who knows whom Dante Alighieri	164
O Love, O you that, for my fealty Cino da Pistoia	55
On the last words of what you write to me Guido Orlandi	61
O poverty, by you the soul is wrapped Guido Cavalcanti	154
O sluggish, hard, ingrate, what do you Guido Cavalcanti	149
O you that often have within your eyes Guido Cavalcanti	37
Right well I know you are Alighieri's son Forese Donati	165
So greatly your great pleasaunce pleasured me Dante da Maiano	43
Song, 'tis my will that you do seek out Love Dante Alighieri	81
Stay now with me, and listen to my sighs Dante Alighieri	119
That lady of all gentle memories Dante Alighieri	123
That star the highest seen in heaven's expanse Dino Frescobaldi	46
The devastating flame of that fierce plague Guido Cavalcanti	54
The dreadful and the desperate hate I bear Cecco Angiolieri	49
The eyes that weep for pity of the heart Dante Alighieri	116
The fountainhead that is so bright to see Guido Cavalcanti	34

The man who feels not, more or less, somewhat Cecco Angiolieri	57
The other night I had a dreadful cough Forese Donati	166
The thoughts are broken in my memory Dante Alighieri	89
The very bitter weeping that you made Dante Alighieri	126
This fairest lady, who, as well I wot Cino da Pistoia	47
This is the damsel by whom love is brought Dino Frescobaldi	45
Though you, indeed, have quite forgotten ruth Guido Cavalcanti	39
Through this my strong and new misaventure Guido Cavalcanti	144
To every heart which the sweet pain does move Dante Alighieri	70
To hear the unlucky wife of Bicci cough Dante Alighieri	165
To sound of trumpet rather than of horn Guido Orlandi	42
To the dim light and the large circle of shade Dante Alighieri	142
Two ladies to the summit of my mind Dante Alighieri	51
Unto that lowly lovely maid, I wis Bernardo da Bologna	33
Upon a day, came Sorrow in to me Dante Alighieri	136
Upon that cruel season when our Lord Onesto di Boncima	146

Vanquished and weary was my soul in me Cino da Pistoia	60
Weep, Lovers, since Love's very self does weep Dante Alighieri	74
What rhymes are yours which I have taken from you Cino da Pistoia	161
Whatever good is naturally done Cecco Angiolieri	27
Whatever while the thought comes over me Dante Alighieri	121
When Lucy draws her mantle round her face Guido Guinicelli	44
Whence come you, all of you so sorrowful Dante Alighieri	145
Whether all grace have failed I scarce may scan Onesto di Boncima	42
Who is she coming, whom all gaze upon Guido Cavalcanti	30
Who utters of his father aught but praise Cecco Angiolieri	50
Whoever without money is in love Cecco Angiolieri	160
Why from the danger did my eyes not start— Guido Cavalcanti	35
Why, if Becchina's heart were diamond Cecco Angiolieri	24
Within a copse I met a shepherd maid Guido Cavalcanti	34
Within the gentle heart Love shelters him Guido Guinicelli	52
With other women I beheld my love— Guido Cavalcanti	29

Woe's me! by dint of all these sighs that come Dante Alighieri	130
Wonderful countenance and royal neck Dante da Maiano	44
Yea, let me praise my lady whom I love Guido Guinicelli	40
You ladies, walking past me piteous-eyed Dante Alighieri	146
You pilgrim-folk, advancing pensively Dante Alighieri	132
You that are wise, let wisdom minister Dante da Maiano	61
You that thus wear a modest countenance Dante Alighieri	99

Glossary

Absalom : son of David
albeit : although
amerce : to fine or penalize arbitrarily
an' : if
Arcidosso and Montegiovi : estates in Tuscany
aught : anything; at all
augury : foretelling the future
bale : injury, suffering
barque or bark : small sailboat; three-master
bate : subtract, lose
Beatrice : Beatrice Portinari; though she died at an early age (24), Dante continued to be fascinated by her.
behoof : advantage, benefit
benison : blessing
Brother Alberts : (?) companions
butt : small cask of wine
clomb : climbed
complaisance : amiability, willingness
concourse : throng; open public space
copse : thicket, small woods
countenance : face, appearance
Croesus : last king of Lydia, known for his wealth; any wealthy person
damsel, damozel : maiden, young woman
decern : adjudge
eke : also; to supplement
emprise : daring, prowess
ere : before

erewhile : a short time ago

erst : a long time ago

fain : inclined to

fealty : faithfulness, pledge, allegiance

florin : gold coin minted in Florence

gainsay : deny, oppose

galley-slave : person chained to an oar in a galley ship

gat : begat, got

ghetto : Jewish quarter; cluster of dwellings for tradesmen, prostitutes, workers

Ghibelline : faction in Florence opposed to the Guelfs; Dante was in the successful Guelf party, then later he was exiled from Florence

glebe : land; parish plot

gramercy : many thanks (from *grand merci*)

groat : four-pence coin

Grosseto : town and province in Tuscany

guerdon : reward

hie : go; go quickly

husbander : manager, head of household

in fee : totally, owning

kirtle : dress or skirt

Lesser Brethren : Catholic sect

Lethe : river of forgetfulness after death

liege, liege slave : loyal subject

Mahomet, Mohammad : prophet of Islam

maize : British term for corn

misaventure : misadventure

natheless : nevertheless

naught, nought : nothing

obeisance : homage, courtesy

pale : picket, stake

pinchbeck : shabby imitation

pleasaunce : private garden, pleasure

prostrate : prone, lying face downward (implying reverence). Does Rossetti mean to say supine?

puissance : power

redound : contribute, return to

ruth : compassion, sorrow, regret

Sarzana : town in Liguria

scapular : loose sleeveless outer garment, such as worn by monks

seigniory : power, as of a lord over an estate

servitor : attendant, servant

shent : chided, cajoled, shamed

sirvent, sirventes : poetic form used by the Troubadour poets; written as satire or parody

smit : smitten, smote; struck

sooth : truth, real

strown : strewn, strewed

teazel, teasel : brush to produce napping on cloth, sometimes with a natural bristle.

thrall : controlled; held in serfdom or slavery

trull : female prostitute, harlot

'twixt : between

vernage : sweet wine

visage : face, appearance

wan : pale

ware : aware

ween : suppose, think

wis : know, suppose

wot : aware of, understand

wrought : made, created

www.ingramcontent.com/pod-product-compliance
Lightning Source LLC
Chambersburg PA
CBHW031353040426
42444CB00005B/277